THE OLIVE TREE

By Aldous Huxley

NOVELS

Eyeless in Gaza
Brave New World
Point Counter Point
Those Barren Leaves
Antic Hay
Crome Yellow

SHORT STORIES

Brief Candles
Two or Three Graces
Little Mexican
Mortal Coils
Limbo

ESSAYS AND BELLES LETTRES

Music at Night
Do What You Will
Proper Studies
Jesting Pilate
Along the Road
On the Margin
Texts and Pretexts
Beyond the Mexique Bay

POETRY

The Cicadas
Leda

SELECT WORKS

Rotunda

THE
OLIVE TREE

by

Aldous Huxley

Harper & Brothers Publishers

NEW YORK AND LONDON

1937

THE OLIVE TREE

Contents

Note

GRATEFUL thanks are due to the following for their kind permission to reprint certain of these essays: To Messrs. Macmillan and Co. Ltd., for "T. H. Huxley as a Literary Man"; to Messrs. William Heinemann Ltd., for the Introduction to "The Letters of D. H. Lawrence"; and to Messrs. Peter Davies Ltd., for "B. R. Haydon."

The essays entitled "Crébillon the Younger" and "In a Tunisian Oasis" were included in the author's "Essays New and Old," published in a limited edition in 1926. The remaining essays in this volume have not previously appeared in book form.

THE OLIVE TREE

Writers and Readers

In Europe and America universal primary education has created a reading public which is practically co-extensive with the adult population. Demand has called forth a correspondingly huge supply: twenty thousand million pounds of wood pulp and esparto grass are annually blackened with printer's ink; the production of newspapers takes rank, in many countries, among the major industries; in English, French and German alone, forty thousand new books are published every year.

A vast activity of writers, a vast and hungry passivity of readers. And when the two come together, what happens? How much and in what ways do the readers respond to the writers? What is the extent, what the limitations, of the influence exercised by writers on their readers? How do extraneous circumstances affect that influence? What are the laws of its waxing and its waning? Hard questions; and the more one thinks about them, the harder they seem. But seeing that they are of intimate concern to all of us (for all of us are readers, with an annual average consumption of probably a million words a year), it will be worth while at least to look for the answers.

The relations existing between scientific writers and their readers are governed by rules agreed upon in advance. So far as we are concerned, there is no problem of scientific literature; and I shall therefore make no further reference to the subject. For the purposes of this analysis, non-scientific writing may be divided into three main classes. In the first we place that vast corpus of literature which is not even intended to have any positive effect upon the reader—all that doughy, woolly, anodyne writing that exists merely to fill a gap of leisure, to kill time and prevent thought, to deaden and diffuse emotion. To a considerable extent reading has become, for almost all of us, an addiction, like cigarette-smoking. We read, most of the time, not because we wish to instruct ourselves, not because we long to have our feelings touched and our imagination fired, but because reading is one of our bad habits, because we suffer when we have time to spare and no printed matter with which to plug the void. Deprived of their newspapers or a novel, reading-addicts will fall back on cookery books, on the literature that is wrapped round bottles of patent medicine, on those instructions for keeping the contents crisp which are printed on the outside of boxes of breakfast cereals. On anything. Of this kind of literature—the literature that exists merely because the second nature of habituated readers abhors a vacuum—it is unnecessary to say more than that there is a great deal of it and that it effectively performs its function.

Into the second class I put the two main types of

propagandist literature—that which aims at modifying the religious and ethical opinions and the personal behaviour of its readers, and that which aims at modifying their social, political and economic opinions and behaviour.

For the sake of convenience, and because it must be given a name, we will call the third class *imaginative literature*. Such literature does not set out to be specifically propagandist, but may none the less profoundly affect its readers' habits of thought, feeling and action.

Let us begin with the propagandists.

What hosts of them there are! All over the world thousands of men and women pass their whole lives denouncing, instructing, commanding, cajoling, imploring their fellows. With what results? One finds it rather hard to say. Most propagandists do their work in the dark, draw bows at a venture. They write; but they don't know how far they will succeed in influencing their readers, nor what are the best means for influencing them, nor how long their influence will last. There is, as yet, no science of propaganda.

This fact may seem the more surprising when we reflect that there is something not far removed from a science of advertising. In the course of years advertisers have come to be fairly expert at selling things to the public. They know accurately enough the potentialities and limitations of different kinds of propaganda —what you can do, for example, by mere statement and repetition; by appeals to such well-organized senti-ments as snobbery and the urge towards social con-formity; by playing on the animal instincts, such as greed, lust and especially fear in all its forms, from the fear of sickness and death to the fear of being ugly, absurd or physically repugnant to one's fellows.

If, then, commercial propagandists know their busi-ness so well, why is it that ethical and political propa-gandists should know theirs on the whole so badly? The answer is that the problems with which the adver-tisers have to deal are fundamentally unlike the prob-lems which confront moralists and, in most cases, poli-ticians. A great deal of advertising is concerned with matters of no importance whatsoever. Thus, I need soap; but it makes not the smallest difference to me whether I buy soap manufactured by X or soap manu-factured by Y. This being so, I can allow myself to be influenced in my choice by such entirely irrelevant considerations as the sex appeal of the girl who smiles so alluringly from X's posters, or the puns and comic drawings on Y's. In many cases, of course, I do not need the commodity at all. But as I have a certain amount of money to spare and am possessed by the strange desire to collect unnecessary objects, I succumb easily to anyone who asks me to buy superfluities and luxuries. In these cases commercial propaganda is an invitation to give in to a natural or acquired craving. In no circumstances does it ever call upon the reader to resist a temptation; always it begs him to succumb. It is not very difficult to persuade people to do what they are all longing to do.

When readers are asked to buy luxuries and super-fluities, or to choose between two brands of the same indispensable necessity, nothing serious is at stake. Advertising is concerned, in these cases, with secondary and marginal values. In other cases, however, it matters or seems to matter a great deal whether the reader allows himself to be influenced by the commercial propagandist or no. Suffering from some pain or physical disability, he is told of the extraordinary cures effected by M's pills or N's lotion. Naturally, he buys at once. In such cases the advertiser has only to make the article persuasively known; the reader's urgent need does the rest.

Ethical and political propagandists have a very different task. The business of the moralist is to persuade people to overcome their egotism and their personal cravings, in the interest either of a supernatural order, or of their own higher selves, or of society. The philosophies underlying the ethical teaching may vary; but the practical advice remains in all cases the same, and this advice is in the main unpleasant; whereas the advice given by commercial propagandists is in the main thoroughly pleasant. There is only one fly in the ointment offered by commercial propagandists; they want your money. Some political propagandists are also

[5]

moralists; they invite their readers to repress their cravings and set limits to their egotistical impulses, to work and suffer for some cause which is to bring happiness in the future. Others demand no personal effort from their readers—merely their adherence to a party, whose success will save the world automatically and, so to speak, from the outside. The first has to persuade people to do something which is on the whole disagreeable. The second has to persuade them of the correctness of a policy which, though it imposes no immediate discomforts, admittedly brings no immediate rewards. Both must compete with other propagandists. The art of political propaganda is much less highly developed than the art of commercial propaganda; it is not surprising.

Long experience has taught the moralists that the mere advertising of virtue is not enough to make people virtuous. During the last few thousands of years, incalculable quantities of hortatory literature have been produced in every civilized country of the world. The moral standard remains, none the less, pretty low. True, if all this ethical propaganda had never been made, the standard might be even lower. We can't tell. I suspect, however, that if we could measure it, we should find that the mechanical efficiency of ethical propaganda through literature was seldom in excess of one per cent. In individual cases and where, for some reason, circumstances are peculiarly favourable, written propaganda may be more efficient than in others. But, in general, if people behave as well as they do, it is not because they have read about good behaviour and the social or metaphysical reasons for being virtuous; it is because they have been subjected, during childhood, to a more or less intensive, more or less systematic training in good behaviour. The propagandists of morality do not rely exclusively or even mainly on the written word.

Unlike the advertisers, political and social propagandists generally work in the dark and are quite uncertain as to the kind of effects they will be able to produce upon their readers. Propagandists themselves seldom admit this fact. Like the rest of us, they like to insist upon their own importance. Moreover, there has been a tendency among historians and political theorists to lend support to their claims. This is not surprising. Being themselves professional writers, historians and political theorists are naturally prone to exaggerate the significance of literature. In most studies of modern history, a great deal of space is devoted to the analysis of different political and economic theories; and it is tacitly or explicitly assumed that the propagation of these theories in the writings of literary men had a more or less decisive influence on the course of history. In other and more reverberant words, the literary men are credited with having "built Nineveh with their sighing and Babel with their mirth." Let us try to discover how far the facts confirm or invalidate this proud claim.

[7]

Consider the propagandist activities of the periodical press. Rich men and politicians have a fixed belief that if they can control the press they will be able to control public opinion—to control it even in a country where democratic institutions are allowed to function without gross interference. They buy up newspapers—partly in order to make money (for the production of newspapers is a very profitable industry), but mainly in the confident hope of being able to persuade the electorate to do what they want it to do. But in fact, as recent history proves, they fail just as often as they succeed. Thus, we see that the electoral successes of the English Liberal Party before the war, and of the Labour Party after, were won in the teeth of opposition by a newspaper press that was and is overwhelmingly conservative. It can be shown by a simple arithmetical calculation that there must be millons of English men and women who regularly read a tory newspaper and regularly vote against the tories. The same is true of France, where it is clear that many readers of the conservative press vote socialist and even communist at elections. We are led to two conclusions: first, that most people choose their daily paper, not for its opinions, but for its entertainingness, its capacity to amuse and fill the vacancies of leisure. Second, that written propaganda is less efficacious than the habits and prejudices, the class loyalties and professional interests of the readers.

Nor must we forget that propaganda is largely at the

[8]

mercy of circumstances. Sometimes circumstances fight against propaganda; at other times, they fight no less effectively on its side. Thus, during the khaki election which returned the first Coalition Government under Lloyd George, and during the gold-standard election of 1931, circumstances fought on the same side as the majority of press propagandists—and fought with tremendous effect. Significant, in this context, is the case of Allied propaganda during the World War. Up till the summer of 1918 the propaganda designed to undermine the will-to-fight of the German troops was almost perfectly ineffective. During and after that summer, when hunger and a series of unsuccessful battles had prepared the ground for it, this propaganda achieved its purpose. But the leaflets which Lord Northcliffe's organization scattered with such good effect during July and August could have done absolutely nothing to discourage the German troops during their victorious offensive against Saint-Quentin in the month of March.

Propaganda by even the greatest masters of style is as much at the mercy of circumstances as propaganda by the worst journalists. Ruskin's diatribes against machinery and the factory system influenced only those who were in an economic position similar to his own; on those who profited by machinery and the factory system they had no influence whatever. From the beginning of the twelfth century to the time of the Council of Trent, denunciations of ecclesiastical and monastic abuses were poured forth almost without inter-mission. And yet, in spite of the eloquence of great writers and great churchmen, like St. Bernard and St. Bonaventura, nothing was done. It needed the circum-stances of the Reformation to produce the counter-Reformation. Upon his contemporaries the influence of Voltaire was enormous. Lucian had as much talent as Voltaire and wrote of religion with the same disinte-grating irony. And yet, so far as we can judge, his writ-ings were completely without effect. The Syrians of the second century were busily engaged in converting themselves to Christianity and a number of other Oriental religions, Lucian's irony fell on ears that were deaf to everything but theology and occultism. In France, during the first half of the eighteenth century, a peculiar combination of historical circumstances had predisposed the educated to a certain religious and po-litical scepticism; people were ready and eager to wel-come Voltaire's attacks on the existing order of things. Political and religious propaganda is effective, it would seem, only upon those who are already partly or entirely convinced of its truth.

Let us consider a modern example. Since the war two well-written and persuasive pieces of propaganda have figured among the very best of best-sellers—I re-fer to Remarque's *All Quiet on the Western Front,* and H. G. Wells's *Outline of History*. In Europe and America many millions of people read the German's

indictment of war and the Englishman's plea for internationalism. With what results? It is hard indeed to
say. All that we can be sure of is that nationalistic feeling was never so acutely inflamed as it is today and the
expenditure on armaments never higher. Once more,
circumstances have been more effective in moulding
men's minds than conscious literary propagandists. The
influence of Wells and Remarque, which was doubtless
considerable at the time of the appearance of their
books, lasted only as long as the post-war disgust with
fighting and the post-war era of prosperity. A new generation, whose members had no first-hand knowledge
of war, came to maturity, and along with it appeared
the great depression. In the desperate effort to preserve
a local prosperity, governments raised tariffs, established
quotas, subsidized exports. Economic nationalism was
everywhere intensified. For every people all foreigners
were automatically transformed into enemies. At the
same time despair and the sense of having been
wronged, of being the victims of a monstrous injustice,
were driving millions to seek consolation and a vicarious triumph in the religion of nationalism. Why, we
may ask in passing, did these unhappy victims of war
choose nationalism as their consolation rather than
Christianity? The reason is to be sought, not in the
superior efficacy of nationalist propaganda, but in the
historical situation as a whole. The prestige of science
is not sufficiently great to induce men to apply scientific

methods to the affairs of social and individual existence; it is great enough, however, to make them reject
the tenets of the transcendental religions. For a large
part of the population, science has made the Christian
dogmas intellectually unacceptable. Contemporary superstition is therefore compelled to assume a positivistic
form. The desire to worship persists, but since modern
men find it impossible to believe in any but observable
entities, it follows that they must vent this desire upon
gods that can be actually seen and heard, or whose existence can at least be easily inferred from the facts of immediate experience. Nations and dictators are only too
clearly observable. It is on these tribal deities that the
longing to worship now vents itself. One of the oddest
and most unexpected results of scientific progress has
been the general reversion from monotheism to local
idolatries. The beginnings of this process are clearly
observable among the German philosophers at the
opening of the nineteenth century. Take a Moravian
Brother; endow him with a great deal of intelligence,
and subject him to a good eighteenth-century education and a first-hand experience of invasion and foreign
tyranny; the result will be a deeply religious man, incapable of finding intellectual satisfaction in the traditional Christianity of his childhood, but ready to pour
out all his devotion, all his will-to-worship, upon the
nation. In a single word, the result will be Fichte. In
Fichte's *Addresses to the German Nation,* the religion

of Nazism is to a great extent anticipated. But whereas the Nazis have invented a jargon of their own, Fichte, it is significant, still employs the language of Pietism. He writes of patriotic experiences in the same words as were used by the Moravians to describe religious experiences. In Fichte, as well as in a number of his less eminent contemporaries, we can actually study an intermediate type between two distinct species—the revivalist Christian and the revivalist nation-worshipper. Since the introduction of universal education innumerable people have gone through a process akin to that which caused Fichte to become dissatisfied with the Pietism of his childhood and made it natural for him to seek another outlet for his will-to-worship. The Napoleonic invasion gave intensity to Fichte's religion of nationalism; defeat and an imperfect victory in the World War have done the same for the Germans and Italians of our own generation. In a word, the historical circumstances of recent years have conspired to intensify nationalism and throw discredit on internationalism, whether religious or political, whether based on Christian theology or a rationalistic view of the world. At the same time, of course, governments have deliberately fostered nationalistic fervour to serve their own political purposes. To these causes must be added the apparently normal human tendency to delight in periodical changes of intellectual and emotional fashion. The very popularity of an author during a certain

[13]

period is a reason why he should become unpopular later on. The conversions due to the preaching of Wells and Remarque were in general superficial and short-lived. It is not to be wondered at.

But now, let us suppose for the sake of argument, that these conversions had been for the most part profound and, in spite of changed conditions, lasting. Would that fact have greatly altered the present situation, so long as the world's rulers had remained unconverted? It is possible to argue that the really influential book is not that which converts ten millions of casual readers, but rather that which converts the very few who, at any given moment, succeed in seizing power. Marx and Sorel have been influential in the modern world, not so much because they were best-sellers (Sorel in particular was not at all a widely read author), but because among their few readers were two men, called respectively Lenin and Mussolini. In a less spectacular way, but still profoundly, the writings of Jeremy Bentham affected the course of nineteenth-century history. Their circulation was not large; but they counted among their readers men like Chadwick, Grote, Romilly, Brougham—administrators, educationists, legal reformers, who did their best to put into practice what Bentham had preached. It may be that the future ruler of some great country will grow up with a passion for Wells. In that case, *The Outline* will be not merely a record of past history, but indirectly a maker of history to come. Up to the present, in spite of its circulation, it has not affected the course of history.

Social and political propaganda, as I have said, is effective, as a rule, only upon those whom circumstances have partly or completely convinced of its truth. In other words, it is influential only when it is a rationalization of the desires, sentiments, prejudices or interests of those to whom it is addressed. A theology or a political theory may be defined as an intellectual device for enabling people to do in cold blood things which, without the theology or the theory, they could only do in the heat of passion. Circumstances, whether external or internal and purely psychological, produce in certain persons a state of discontent, for example, a desire for change, a passionate aspiration for something new. These emotional states may find occasional outlet in violent but undirected activity. But now comes the writer with a theology or a political theory, in terms of which these vague feelings can be rationalized. The energy developed by the prevailing passions of the masses is given a direction and at the same time strengthened and made continuous. Sporadic outbursts are converted by the rationalization into purposive and unremitting activity. The mechanism of successful propaganda may be roughly summed up as follows. Men accept the propagandist's theology or political theory, because it apparently justifies and explains the sentiments and desires evoked in them by the circum-

[15]

stances. The theory may, of course, be completely absurd from a scientific point of view; but this is of no importance so long as men believe it to be true. Having accepted the theory, men will work in obedience to its precepts even in times of emotional tranquillity. Moreover, the theory will often cause them to perform in cold blood acts which they would hardly have performed even in a state of emotional excitement.

Our nature abhors a moral and intellectual vacuum. Passion and self-interest may be our chief motives; but we hate to admit the fact even to ourselves. We are not happy unless our acts of passion can be made to look as though they were dictated by reason, unless self-interest be explained and embellished so as to seem to be idealistic. Particular grievances call not only for redress, but also for the formulation of universally valid reasons why they should be redressed. Particular cravings cry aloud to be legitimized in terms of a rational philosophy and a traditionally acceptable ethic. The moral and intellectual vacuum is perpetually in process of formation, and it sucks into itself whatever explanatory or justificatory writing happens at the moment to be available. Clean or dirty, brackish or sweet—any water will serve the turn of a pump that has been emptied of its air. And, analogously, any philosophical writing, good, bad or indifferent, will serve the turn of people who are under the compulsion of desire or of self-interest, and who consequently feel the need of intellectual and moral justification. Hence the extraordinary success, at a particular historical moment, of books that, to a later generation, seem almost completely valueless; hence the temporary importance and power of manifestly second-rate and negligible writers. Let us consider a concrete example. The organization of eighteenth-century French society was hopelessly inefficient, and its pattern so anachronistic that great numbers of individual Frenchmen, unable to fit into the scheme of things, suffered acute discomfort. The sense of grievance and the desire for change were intense; and correspondingly intense was the desire for a philosophy that should rationalize this desire and legitimize this grievance in terms of pure reason and absolute justice. Yearning to be filled, the moral and intellectual vacuum sucked into itself whatever writings were available. Among these was the *De l'Esprit* of Helvétius. This is a thoroughly bad book, full of preposterous stuff. But though obviously untrue, some of its theses (such as that which affirmed the equality of all intellects and the consequent possibility of transforming any child at will into a Newton or a Raphael) were well suited to rationalize and justify the contemporary claims for political, religious and economic reform. During a few years the book was invested with a significance, and exercised an influence, which its intrinsic literary and philosophical merits could not justify. Its fortune was made, not by the ability of its author, but by the needs of its readers.

There have been writers whose influence depended neither on their own powers, nor yet on the necessities of their readers, but simply upon fashion. To us, the writings of most of the original fourteenth- and fifteenth-century humanists seem wholly unreadable. Nor are we singular in our judgment; for within a hundred years their works had fallen into an almost complete oblivion. And yet, for their contemporaries, these works were exciting and persuasive. The fact that a man could turn out a tolerably specious imitation of Cicero or Sallust was, for two whole generations of Renaissance readers, a sufficient reason for attaching importance to what he wrote. Gian Galeazzo Visconti of Milan was often heard to say that a thousand Florentine cavalry could not do him so much harm as a single Latin letter from the Chancellor of Florence, the humanist Coluccio Salutati. The rediscovery of ancient literature was an event of profound significance. It is easy to understand why so much importance came to be attached, during the fifteenth century, to pure Latinity: why it was that scholars like Valla and Poggio should have wielded such extraordinary power. But the fashion which, a century later, invested the ruffianly Pietro Aretino with the almost magical prestige that had belonged to the original humanists is wholly unaccountable. Aretino was a lively writer, some of whose works

[18]

can still be read with interest. But why he should have wielded the influence that he did, and why all the kings and princes in Europe should have thought it worth while to pay him blackmail, are mysteries which we cannot explain, except by saying that for some reason he became the mode.

At every period of history certain writings are regarded by all or some members of a given society as being *ex hypothesi* true. They are therefore charged with an unquestionable authority. To show that this authority is on the side of the cause he supports has always been one of the propagandist's tasks. Where it is not possible for him to make them serve his purposes the propagandist has to discredit the existing authorities. The devil opens the attack by quoting Scripture; then, when the quotations fail him, trots out the Higher Criticism and shows that Scripture has no more authority than the *Pickwick Papers*. At any given moment there are certain fixed landmarks of authority; the propaganda of the period has to orientate itself in relation to these landmarks. Correct orientation to existing authority is one of the conditions making for success of propaganda.

We see, then, that the effectiveness of propaganda is determined by the circumstances of the time when it is written. These circumstances are of two kinds—circumstances external to the individual, and internal or psychological circumstances. External circumstances

[19]

may change catastrophically, as during a war; or gradually, as when means of production are altered and economic prosperity is increased or diminished. Changes in external circumstances are, of course, accompanied by changes in internal circumstances. But internal circumstances may also change on their own account, independently, to a certain extent, of external circumstances and according to an autonomous rhythm of their own. History pursues an undulatory course; and these undulations are the result, to some extent at least, of the tendency displayed by human beings to react, after a certain time, away from the prevailing habits of thought and feeling towards other habits. (This process is greatly complicated by the fact that in modern heterogeneous societies there are numerous co-existing groups with different habits of thought and feeling. But it is unnecessary to discuss these complications here.) The autonomous nature of psychological undulations is confirmed by the facts of history. Thus the ardour of all violently active religious and political movements has generally given place to relative indifference and worldliness after a period of anything from a few months to twenty-five years.

"All active religions," writes Professor Crane Brinton, in the concluding paragraph of his recently published *Decade of Revolution*, "tend to become inactive within a generation at most. The wise, experienced and consistently inactive religious institution known as the

Roman Catholic Church has always been threatened
by outbreaks of active religion. Until Luther, at least,
such outbreaks were tamed, strait-jacketed with laws
and institutions. . . . Since the Reformation the great
outbreaks of active religion have taken place outside the
Church of Rome. Of these, the earliest, Calvinism, has
long since been sobered. . . . The second, Jacobinism,
has in the Third Republic made its compromise with
the flesh. . . . The third, Marxism, would appear to
the outsider to be entering the inactive stage, at least
in Russia." It is worth while to illustrate the undulations of history by a few concrete examples. It took
the Franciscan movement about twenty years to lose
the passion of its early zeal. Francis founded his first
cell in 1209, and the Bull by which Gregory IX set aside
his Testament and permitted trustees to hold and ad-
minister property for the benefit of the Order was
promulgated in 1230. The French Revolution had its
Thermidorean reaction after only five years, Savonarola
ruled the city of Florence for eight years; but the popular reaction against his movement of religious and
moral reform had begun some time before the end.
The great Kentucky Revival lasted from 1797 to about
1805; but the Welsh Revival of 1904 was over in two
years.

It is probably true to say that movements make up
in duration what they lack in intensity. Thus, it seems
to have taken a full generation for educated English-

men to react away from the genteel religious scepticism
which prevailed at the beginning of the eighteenth century. Addison complained that in his time the very
appearances of Christianity had vanished; Leibniz
could record the fact that in England even "natural religion" was languishing. And these are opinions which
the facts confirm. The literature of unbelief was as
popular as fiction. For example, Woolston's Discourses
against miracles sold upwards of thirty thousand copies.
But a change was at hand. In a letter dated 1776 and
addressed to Gibbon on the publication of the first
volume of his history, Hume summed up his impres-
sions of contemporary English thought in the following
words: "Among many other marks of decline, the prev-
alence of superstition in England prognosticates the fall
of philosophy and decay of taste." Fourteen years later,
in 1790, Burke remarked that "not one man born
within the last forty years has read a word of Collins,
Toland, Tyndal, or of any of that flock of so-called free-
thinkers. Atheism is not only against our reason; it is
against our instinct." Forty years is probably a pretty
accurate computation. Charles Wesley was converted in
1736 and John in 1738. By 1750 the movement of
which those conversions were at once a symptom and
a cause must have gone far enough to spoil the market
for deistic literature. After several minor fluctuations, a
new period of educated scepticism set in about the middle of the nineteenth century and was succeeded to-

wards the end of the century by another reaction towards faith. Owing, however, to the assaults of nineteenth-century rationalism, this new faith could not be exclusively Christian or transcendental in character, but expressed itself in terms of a variety of pseudo-religious forms, of which the most important was nationalism. Rudyard Kipling was the early twentieth-century equivalent of Cardinal Newman and Wesley. The mistake of all propagandists has been to suppose that the psychological movement which they observe in the society around them is destined to go on continuously in the same direction. Thus we see that in a time of scepticism, sceptical propagandists announce with triumph that superstition is dead and reason triumphant. In a time of religious reaction, Christian and nationalistic propagandists announce with equal satisfaction and certainty that scepticism has for ever been destroyed. Both, it is hardly necessary to say, are wrong. The course of history is undulatory, because (among other reasons) self-conscious men and women easily grow tired of a mode of thought and feeling which has lasted for more than a certain time. Propaganda gives force and direction to the successive movements of popular feeling and desire; but it does not do much to create those movements. The propagandist is a man who canalizes an already existing stream. In a land where there is no water, he digs in vain.

In a democratic state, any propagandist will have

rivals competing with him for the support of the public. In totalitarian states there is no liberty of expression for writers and no liberty of choice for their readers. There is only one propagandist—the State.

That all-powerful rulers who make a regular use of terrorism should also be the most active propagandists known to history seems at first sight paradoxical. But you can do anything with bayonets except sit on them. Even a despot cannot govern for any length of time without the consent of his subjects. Dictatorial propaganda aims first of all at the legitimizing in popular estimation of the dictator's government. Old-established governments do not need to produce certificates of legitimacy. Long habit makes it seem "natural" to people that they should be ruled by an absolute or constitutional monarch, by a republican president, by a prince bishop, by an oligarchy of senatorial families— whichever the case may be. New rulers have to prove that they have not usurped their title, but possess some higher right to govern than the mere fact of having grabbed power. Usurpation, like any other crime, has to justify itself in terms of the prevailing code of values —in terms, that is to say, of the very system which brands it as a crime. For example, in Italy during the fourteenth and fifteenth centuries there were two acknowledged sources of political power: the Empire and the Church. For this reason the men who had succeeded, by fraud or violence, in seizing the government

of a city, generally hastened to have themselves appointed Vicars of the Church or Hereditary Captains of
the Empire. To be able to tyrannize effectively they
needed the title and appearance of constitutional authority. Since the French Revolution the recognized
sources of power have been the People and the Nation.
When modern despots have to legitimize their usurpa-
tions they do so in terms of nationalism and of that
humanitarian democracy they themselves have over-
thrown. They issue propaganda to prove that their
regime is for the good of the people or else, if the economic facts make nonsense of such a claim, for the
good of that mystical entity, different from and superior
to the mere individuals composing it, the Nation. But
the general acknowledgment that his government is
legitimate is not enough for the totalitarian dictator;
he demands from his subjects that they shall all think
and feel alike, and he uses every device of propaganda
in order to make them think and feel alike. Complete
psychological homogeneity occurs among primitive peoples. But the conditions of such homogeneity are, first,
that the population shall be small; secondly, that it
shall live in an isolation due either to geography or to
the exclusiveness of the local religion; and, thirdly, that
its system of production shall be more or less completely
unspecialized. European dictators may wish and try to
make their peoples as homogeneous as a tribe of
Melanesians, to impose upon them a conformity as

[25]

complete as that which exists among the Australian aborigines. But circumstances must finally prove too strong for them. Fifty million professionally specialized men and women cannot live together without emphasizing one another's natural diversities. Nor, with the best will in the world, can the dictator isolate himself from all contact with the outside world. This is one of the reasons why, in the long run, he is bound to fail. Meanwhile, he is sure of at least a partial and temporary success. Dictatorial propaganda demands obedience and even considerable financial and other sacrifices; but by way of compensation it assures the individual that, as a member of a chosen nation, race, or class, he is superior to all other individuals in the world; it dissipates his sense of personal inferiority by investing him with the vicarious glory of the community; it gives him reasons for thinking well of himself, it provides him with enemies whom he may blame for his own shortcomings and upon whom he may vent his latent brutality and love of bullying. Commercial propaganda is acceptable, because it encourages men and women to satisfy their sensuous cravings and offers them escapes from their physical pains and discomforts. Dictatorial propaganda, which is always nationalistic or revolutionary propaganda, is acceptable because it encourages men and women to give free rein to their pride, vanity and other egotistical tendencies, and because it provides them with psychological devices for overcoming their sense

[26]

of personal inferiority. Dictatorial propaganda promotes the ugly reality of prejudice and passion to the rank of an ideal. Dictators are the popes of nationalism; and the creed of nationalism is that what ought to be is merely what is, only a good deal more so. All individuals seek justifications for such passions as envy, hatred, avarice and cruelty; by means of nationalistic and revolutionary propaganda, dictators provide them with such justifications. It follows, therefore, that this propaganda of the dictators is certain to enjoy a certain temporary popularity. In the long run, as I have said, the impossibility of reducing a huge, educated population to the spiritual homogeneity of a savage tribe will tell against it. Furthermore, human beings have a strong tendency towards rationality and decency. (If they had not, they would not desire to legitimize their prejudices and their passions.) A doctrine that identifies what ought to be with the lowest elements of actual reality cannot remain acceptable for long. Finally, policies based upon a tribal morality simply won't work in the modern world. The danger is that, in process of proving that they don't work, the dictators may destroy that world.

Dictatorial propaganda may be classified under two heads: negative and positive. Positive propaganda consists of all that is written, negative propaganda, of all that is not written. In all dictatorial propaganda, silence is at least as important as speech, *suppressio veri*

[27]

as *suggestio falsi*. Indeed, the negative propaganda of silence is probably more effective as an instrument of persuasion and mental regimentation than speech. Silence creates the conditions in which such words as are spoken or written take most effect.

An excess of positive propaganda evokes boredom and exasperation in the minds of those to whom it is addressed. Advertising experts are well aware that, after a certain point, an increase in the pressure of salesmanship produces rapidly diminishing and finally negative returns. What is true of commercial propaganda seems to be equally true, in this respect, of political propaganda. Thus, most observers agree that at the Danzig elections, the Nazi propagandists harmed their cause by "protesting too much." Danzig, however, was a free city; the opposition was allowed to speak and the ground had not been prepared for positive propaganda by a preliminary course of silence and suppression. What are the effects of excessive positive propaganda within the totalitarian state? Reliable evidence is not available. Significant, however, in this context is the decline, since the advent of Nazism, in the circulation of German newspapers. Protesting too much and all in the same way, the propagandists succeeded only in disgusting their readers. *Suppressio veri* has one enormous advantage over *suggestio falsi*: in order to say nothing, you do not have to be a great stylist. People may get bored with positive propaganda; but where negative propaganda is so effective that there is no alternative to the spoken and written suggestions that come to them, all but the most independent end by accepting those suggestions.

The propagandists of the future will probably be chemists and physiologists as well as writers. A cachet containing three-quarters of a gramme of chloral and three-quarters of a milligram of scopolamine will produce in the person who swallows it a state of complete psychological malleability, akin to the state of a subject under deep hypnosis. Any suggestion made to the patient while in this artificially induced trance penetrates to the very depths of the sub-conscious mind and may produce a permanent modification in the habitual modes of thought and feeling. In France, where the technique has been in experimental use for several years, it has been found that two or three courses of suggestion under chloral and scopolamine can change the habits even of the victims of alcohol and irrepressible sexual addictions. A peculiarity of the drug is that the amnesia which follows it is retrospective; the patient has no memories of a period which begins several hours *before* the drug's administrations. Catch a man unawares and give him a cachet; he will return to consciousness firmly believing all the suggestions you have made during his stupor and wholly unaware of the way this astonishing conversion has been effected. A system of propaganda, combining pharmacology with literature, should be completely and infallibly effective. The thought is extremely disquieting.

So far, I have dealt with the influence exercised by writers who wish to persuade their readers to adopt some particular kind of social or political attitude. We must now consider the ways in which writers influence readers as private individuals. The influence of writers in the sphere of personal thought, feeling and behaviour is probably even more important than their influence in the sphere of politics. But the task of defining that influence or of exactly assessing its amount is one of extraordinary difficulty. "Art," it has been said, "is the forgiveness of sins." In the best art we perceive persons, things and situations more clearly than in life and as though they were in some way more real than realities themselves. But this clearer perception is at the same time less personal and egotistic. Writers who permit their readers to see in this intense but impersonal way exercise an influence which, though not easily definable, is certainly profound and salutary.

Works of imaginative literature have another and more easily recognizable effect; by a kind of suggestion they modify the characters of those who read them. The French philosopher, Jules de Gaultier, has said that one of the essential faculties of the human being is "the power granted to man to conceive himself as other than he is." He calls this power "bovarism" after the heroine of Flaubert's novel Madame Bovary. To some extent all men and women live under false names, are disguised as someone else, assume, whether consciously or unconsciously, a borrowed character. This *persona*, as Jung calls it, is formed to a great extent by a process of imitation. Sometimes the imitation is of living human beings, sometimes of fictional or historic characters; sometimes of virtuous and socially desirable personages, sometimes of criminals and adventurers. It may be, in the significant phrase of Thomas à Kempis, the Imitation of Christ; or it may be the imitation of the heroines of Mr. Michael Arlen's novels; the imitation of Julius Caesar or of the Buddha; of Mussolini or Werther; of Stavrogin or Sainte Thérèse de Lisieux or the gunmen of penny dreadfuls. People have bovarized themselves into the likeness of every kind of real or imaginary being. Sometimes the imitator chooses a model fairly like himself; but it also happens that he chooses one who is profoundly dissimilar. What de Gaultier calls the bovaric angle between reality and assumed *persona* may be wide or narrow. In extreme cases the bovaric angle can be equal to two right angles. In other words, the real and assumed characters may have exactly opposite tendencies. Most of us, I imagine, go through life with a bovaric angle of between forty-five and ninety degrees.

Teachers have always tried to exploit the bovaric tendencies of their pupils, and the historical and literary model for imitation has from time immemorial played an important part in all moral education. Like other propagandists, however, educators are still unable to foresee how their pupils will respond to moral propaganda. Sometimes the response is positive, sometimes negative. We do not yet know enough to say, in any given circumstances, which it will be. The influence of books is certainly very great; but nobody, least of all their writers, can say in advance who will be influenced, or in what way, or for how long. The extreme form of bovarism is paranoia. Here the individual plays a part so wholeheartedly that he comes to believe that he actually *is* the character he is impersonating. The influence of books on paranoiacs must be very considerable. People suffering from the paranoia of persecution often imagine that they are the victims of a diabolical secret society, which is identified with some real organization, such as that of the Freemasons or the Jesuits, about which the patient has read in history books or perhaps in works of fiction. In cases of the paranoia of ambition, books certainly serve to canalize the patient's madness. Megalomaniacs believe themselves to be divine or royal personages, or descendants of great historical figures, of whom they can have heard only in books. There is material here for an interesting medico-literary study.

Incidentally it may be remarked that many authors are themselves mildly paranoid in character. Books become popular because they vicariously satisfy a common wish. In many cases, also, they are written with the aim of satisfying the author's secret wishes, of realizing, if only in words, his bovaristic dreams. Consult a library catalogue and you will find that more books have been written on the career of Napoleon than on any other single subject. This fact casts a strange and rather terrifying light on the mentality of modern European writers and readers. How are we going to get rid of war, so long as people find their keenest bovaristic satisfaction in the story of the world's most spectacular militarist?

The course of psychological history is undulatory; therefore it happens that the literary models most commonly imitated at one period lose their popularity with succeeding generations. Thus, in the early eighteenth century, what Englishman or Frenchman would have desired to imitate those monsters of honour, who figured in the romances and plays of the later sixteenth and earlier seventeenth centuries? And who at the same period would have dreamed of assuming the sentimental rôles so popular after about 1760? In a majority of cases readers choose to play the parts that come easiest to them. Thus it is obviously extremely difficult to act the part of a saint. For this reason the New Testament, though more widely read in Europe and over a longer period than any other book, has produced relatively few successful imitators of its central character. People have always preferred to play parts that would allow them to satisfy their appetites or their will to power. As in the time of Paolo and Francesca, the favourite heroes are still personages like Lancelot—great warriors and great lovers.

> Quando leggemmo il disiato riso
>   esser baciato da cotanto amante,
>   questi, che mai da me non fia diviso,
> la bocca mi baciò tutto tremante.
>   Galeotto fu il libro e chi lo scrisse;
>   quel giorno più non vi leggemmo avante.

Dante provides us with a perfect example of erotic bovarism actively at work.

Certain fictional personages continue to make their appeal even over long periods and through considerable fluctuations in the habits of thought and feeling. Stendhal's Julien Sorel, for example, is still alive in France; and I was interested to learn from a Communist friend that this exemplar of ruthless individualism had recently achieved a great popularity in Russia. The vitality of Hamlet after more than three hundred years remains so great that the Nazis have found it necessary to discountenance revivals of the tragedy for fear that it should cause young Germans to forget the "heroic" rôle which they are now supposed to play.

It sometimes happens that writers who are without influence on the habits of thought and feeling of their contemporaries begin to exercise such an influence after their death, when circumstances have so changed as to make their doctrine more acceptable. Thus, William Blake's peculiar sexual mysticism did not come into its own until the twentieth century. Blake died in 1827; but in a certain sense he was a contemporary of D. H. Lawrence. Along with Lawrence, he exercised a considerable influence over many people in post-war England and elsewhere. Whether the nature of this influence was what either Blake or Lawrence would have liked it to be is extremely doubtful. In a majority of cases, we may suspect, the mystical doctrines of Blake and Lawrence were used by their readers merely as a justification for a desire to indulge in the maximum amount of sexual promiscuity with a minimum amount of responsibility. That Lawrence passionately disapproved of such a use being made of his writings, I know; and it is highly probable that Blake would have shared his feelings. It is one of the ironies of the writer's fate that he can never be quite sure what sort of influence he will have upon his readers. Lawrence's books, as we have seen, were used as justifications for sexual promiscuity. For this reason they were outlawed by the Nazis when they first came into power, as mere *Schmutzliteratur*. Now, it appears, the Nazis have changed their minds about Lawrence; and his writings are accepted as justifications for violence, anti-rationalism, idolatry and the worship of blood. That Lawrence meant to make his readers turn from intellectualism and conscious emotionalism towards the Dark Gods of instinct and physiology, is unquestionable. But it is safe to say that he did not mean to turn them into Nazis. Men are influenced by books to assume a character that is not entirely their own; but the character they assume may be quite different from the character idealized by the writer.

Even propagandists may achieve results quite unlike those they meant to achieve by their writings. For example, by persistently attacking an institution authors hope to persuade either its supporters or its victims to reform it. But in practice they may just as easily produce a precisely opposite effect. For invectives often act as a kind of vaccination against the danger of reform. Mr. Shaw's writings are revolutionary in intention, and yet he has become a favourite among the more intelligent members of the bourgeoisie; they read his satires and denunciations, laugh at themselves a little, decide that it's all really too bad; then, feeling that they have paid the tribute which capitalism owes to social justice, close the book and go on behaving as they have always behaved. The works of revolutionary writers may serve as prophylactics against revolution. Instead of producing the active will to change, they produce cynicism, which is the acceptance of things as they are, combined with the derisive knowledge that they couldn't be worse—a knowledge that is felt by the person who possesses it to excuse him from making any personal effort to change the intolerable situation.

Cynicism can affect not only those who profit by the existence of an undesirable state of things, but also those who are its victims. During the centuries which preceded the Reformation, cynical acceptance of the evils of ecclesiastical corruption was common among those who paid the piper as well as among those who called the tune, among the intelligent laity as well as among the princes of the Church. The fact of corruption was accepted as inevitable, like bad weather—a kind of bad weather that was at the same time a joke. Boccaccio, Chaucer, Poggio and their lesser contemporaries denounced, but at the same time they laughed. Poggio's employers at the Vatican (he was a papal secretary) laughed with them. At a later date Erasmus's ecclesiastical and princely friends laughed no less heartily over his satirical comments on kings and clerics. So did all the rest of the reading public. For Erasmus was, for his period, a prodigious best-seller. The Paris edition of his *Colloquies* sold twenty-four thousand copies in a few weeks—an incredibly large figure, when one reflects that the book was written in Latin. Of his *Praise of Folly* a hundred editions were printed between 1512 and 1676—most of them during the earlier part of that period.

After Luther had taken his revolutionary action, and when it had become clear that the movement for reform was a serious menace to the existing order of things, the official attitude towards Erasmus's writings began to change. In 1528 the *Colloquies* were suppressed, as being dangerously subversive. From fosterers of an amused acceptance and prophylactics against revolution, his denunciatory and satirical writings had been transformed, by the new circumstances, into dangerous revolutionary propaganda. Erasmus's failure to achieve what he meant to achieve was doubly complete. He meant to persuade the existing hierarchy to reform itself; he only succeeded in making it cynically laugh at itself. Then came Luther; and the writings which their author had penned as propaganda for rational reform within the Church were transformed automatically into propaganda for a revolution, of which he disapproved. And when the Church did reform itself, it was not at all in the Erasmian way. But luckily for Erasmus, he was not there to witness that reformation. Three years before the Society of Jesus came into the world the old humanist had passed out of it—none too early.

Let us return to our imaginative literature. Readers, as we have seen, often borrow characters from books in order to use them, bovaristically, in real life. But they also reverse this process and, projecting themselves out of reality into literature, live a compensatory life of fantasy between the lines of print. One of the main functions of all popular fiction, drama and now the cinema has been to provide people with the means of assuaging, vicariously and in fancy, their unsatisfied longings, with the psychological equivalents

of stimulants and narcotics. The power of such literature to impose upon those whom we may call it ad-
dicts a kind of drugged acceptance of even the most
sordid realities is probably very considerable. In real
life one Englishman out of every sixty thousand is a
peer, one out of every three hundred thousand has an
income of a hundred thousand pounds a year. A cen-
sus of fictional characters has never, so far as I know,
been made; but I should guess that one out of a
hundred, perhaps even one out of fifty; was either a
lord, or a millionaire, or both at once. The presence of
so many aristocrats and plutocrats in our literature has
two causes. The first is that the rich and powerful
enjoy more liberty than the poor and so are in a
position to make their own tragedies, not merely to
have disaster forced upon them from outside. There
can be no drama without personal choice; and, pro-
verbially, beggars cannot be choosers. Only people
with incomes can afford to do much choosing in this
world. "Their rich and noble souls" (to quote one of
Butler's Erewhonian authors) "can defy all material
impediment; whereas the souls of the poor are clogged
and hampered by matter, which sticks fast about them
as treacle to the wings of a fly. . . . This is the secret
of the homage which we see rich men receive from
those who are poorer than themselves." Of the homage,
too, that they receive from authors. The rich, the
powerful and the talented are freer than ordinary folk
and are therefore the predestined subjects of imagina-

[39]

tive literature. The other reason why literature is so
lavish with wealth and titles is to be sought in the
very fact that the real world is so niggardly of these
things. Authors themselves and their readers desire
imaginary compensations for their poverty and social
insignificance. In the lordly and gilded world of literature they get it. Nor are poverty and powerlessness
their only troubles; it is more than likely that they are
also plain, have an insufficient or unromantic sex life;
are married and wish they weren't, or unmarried and
wish they were; are too old or too young; in a word,
are themselves and not somebody else. Hence those
Don Juans, those melting beauties, those innocent
young kittens, those beautifully brutal boys, those
luscious adventuresses. Hence Hollywood, hence the
beauty chorus. When I was last at Margate a gigantic
new movie palace had just been opened. Its name implied a whole social programme, a complete theory of
art; it was called "Dreamland." At the present time,
the cinema acts far more effectively as the opium of the
people than does religion.

Hitherto I have described the more obvious effects
produced by imaginative literature upon its readers.
But it works also less conspicuously and in subtler ways:

Who prop, thou ask'st, in these bad days, my mind? . . .
He much, the old man, who, clearest-soul'd of men,
Saw The Wide Prospect and the Asian Fen,
And Tmolus hill, and Smyrna bay, though blind. . . .

[40]

And, in *The Waste Land*, Mr. Eliot uses the same metaphor:

> O swallow swallow
> Le Prince d'Aquitaine à la tour abolie
> These fragments I have shored against my ruins
> When then Ile fit you. Hieronymo's mad againe
> Datta, Dayadhvam, Damyata.
>   Shantih shantih shantih.

Words have power to support, to buttress, to hold together. And are at the same time moulds, into which we pour our own thought—and it takes their nobler and more splendid form—at the same time channels and conduits into which we divert the stream of our being—and it flows significantly towards a comprehensible end. They prop, they give form and direction to our experience. And at the same time they themselves provide experience of a new kind, intense, pure, unalloyed with irrelevance. Words expressing desire may be more moving than the presence of the desired person. The hatred we feel at the sight of our enemies is often less intense than the hatred we feel when we read a curse or an invective. In words men find a new universe of thought and feeling, clearer and more comprehensible than the universe of daily experience. The verbal universe is at once a mould for reality and a substitute for it, a superior reality. And what props the mind, what shores up its impending ruin, is contact with this superior reality of ordered beauty and significance.

In the past the minds of cultured Europeans were shaped and shored up by the Bible and the Greek and Latin classics. Men's philosophy of life tended to crystallize itself in phrases from the Gospels or the Odes of Horace, from the Iliad or the Psalms. Job and Sappho, Juvenal and the Preacher gave style to their despairs, their loves, their indignations, their cynicisms. Experience taught them the wisdom that flowed along verbal channels prepared by Aeschylus and Solomon; and the existence of these verbal channels was itself an invitation to learn wisdom from experience. To-day most of us resemble Shakespeare in at least one important respect; we know little Latin and less Greek. Even the Bible is rapidly becoming, if not a closed, at any rate a very rarely opened book. The phrases of the Authorized Version no longer prop and mould and canalize our minds. St. Paul and the Psalmist have gone the way of Virgil and Horace. What authors have taken their place? Whose words support contemporary men and women? The answer is that there exists no single set of authoritative books. The common ground of all the Western cultures has slipped away from under our feet.

Locally authoritative literatures are filling the vacuum created by the virtual disappearance from the modern consciousness of those internationally authoritative literatures which dominated men's minds in the past.

Mein Kampf is a gospel and has had a sale comparable to that of the Bible—two million copies in ten years. For Russians, Marx and Lenin have become what Aristotle was for educated Europeans in the thirteenth century. (Lenin's works, in twenty-seven volumes, have already sold four million sets.) In Italy *Mussolini ha sempre ragione*; no higher claim was made by the orthodox for Moses or the Evangelists.

The peoples of the West no longer share a literature and a system of ancient wisdom. All that they now have in common is science and information. Now, science is knowledge, not wisdom; deals with quantities, not with the qualities of which we are immediately aware. In so far as we are enjoying and suffering beings, its words seem to us mostly irrelevant and beside the point. Moreover, these words are arranged without art; therefore possess no magical power and are incapable of propping or moulding the mind of the reader.

The same is true of that other bond of union between the peoples, shared information. The disseminators of information often try to write with the compulsive magic of art; but how rarely they succeed! It is not with fragments of the daily paper that we shore up our ruins.

The literature of information has, as its subject-matter, events which people feel to be humanly relevant. Unfortunately, journalism treats these profoundly interesting themes in what is, for all its flashing brilliance, a profoundly uninteresting, superficial way. Moreover, its business is to record history from day to day; it can never afford to linger over any particular episode. As little can the reader afford to linger. Even if the daily paper were well written, its very dailiness would preclude the possibility of his remembering any part of its contents. Materially, a thing of printer's ink and wood pulp, a newspaper does not outlast the day of its publication; by sunset it is in the dust-bin or the cesspool. In the reader's memory its contents survive hardly so long. Nobody who reads—as well as all the rest—two or three papers a day can possibly be expected to remember what is in them. Yesterday's news is chased out of mind by to-day's. We remember what we read several times and with intense concentration. It was thus, because they were authoritative and had a mysterious prestige, that the Bible and the Greek and Latin classics were read. It is not thus that we read the *Daily Mail* or the *Petit Parisien*.

In modern scientific method we have a technique for invention; technological progress proceeds at an accelerating speed. But social change is inevitably associated with technological progress. To quicken the rate of the second is to quicken the rate of the first. The subject-matter of the literature of information has been enormously increased and has become more disquietingly significant than ever before. At the same time improvements in the technique for supplying information have created a demand for information. Our tendency is to attach an ever-increasing importance to news and to that quality of last-minute contemporaneity which invests even certain works of art, even certain scientific hypotheses and philosophical speculations, with the glamour of a political assassination or a Derby result. Accustomed as we are to devouring information, we make a habit of reading a great deal very rapidly. There must be many people who, once having escaped from school or the university, never read anything with concentration or more than once. They have no verbal props to shore against their ruins. Nor, indeed, do they need any props. A mind that is sufficiently pulverized and sufficiently agitated supports itself by the very violence of its motion. It ceases to be a ruin and becomes a whirling sandstorm.

In a certain sense our passion for information defeats its own object, which is increased knowledge of the world and other human beings. We are provided with a vastly greater supply of facts than our ancestors ever had an opportunity of considering. And yet our knowledge of other peoples is probably less thorough and intimate than theirs. In 1500 an educated Frenchman or German knew very little about current political events in England and nothing at all of the activities, so lavishly recorded in our literature of information, of English criminals, aristocrats, sportsmen, actresses. Nevertheless, he probably knew more about the intimate intellectual and emotional processes of English-

men than his better-informed descendants know to-day.
This knowledge was derived from introspection. Knowing himself he knew them. Minds moulded by the same
religious and secular literatures were in a position to
understand one another in a way which is inconceivable
to men who have in common only science and information. By discrediting the Bible and providing a more
obviously useful substitute for the study of the dead
languages, triumphant science has completed the work
of spiritual disunion which was begun when it under-
mined belief in transcendental religion and so prepared
the way for the positivistic superstitions of nationalism
and dictator-worship. It remains to be seen whether it
will discover a way to put this shattered Humpty-
Dumpty together again.

T. H. Huxley as a Literary Man*

MR. G. K. CHESTERTON has a genius for saying new and surprising things about old subjects. We are grateful to him for his originality. But there is such a thing as being too original by half; and it sometimes happens that what Mr. Chesterton says is so new and so surprising that it has very little perceptible relevance to the subject under discussion. For example, in that stimulating little book, *The Victorian Age in Literature*, he says of Lord Macaulay and T. H. Huxley that "they were both much more under the influence of their own admirable rhetoric than they knew. Huxley, especially, was much more a literary than a scientific man."

Well, this is new and surprising enough—new and surprising, indeed, to the point of being quite untrue. The records of Huxley's scientific achievements are there to prove the contrary. He was a man of science first of all—a man of science who also had, what quite a number of men of science before and after his day have had, a literary gift.

Being myself of the literary profession, I think I can guess how a fellow man of letters would arrive at the conclusion so boldly enunciated in Mr. Chesterton's book. The process is simplicity itself. All that is re-

* Delivered as the Huxley Memorial Lecture, 1932.

[47]

quired is a little systematic and selective ignorance. Ostrich-like, one shuts one's eyes to the scientific achievements of one's subject. One refrains from reading any of his technical papers (and, incidentally, even if one did read them, one would not understand them) ; and one concentrates exclusively on his more accessible, his more specifically literary productions. The result is that one comes, logically and inevitably, to the conclusion that "Huxley, especially, was much more a literary than a scientific man." Q.E.D. It is as evident as a proposition of Euclid.

It would be easy to apply the same process to other men of science and to arrive at exactly similar conclusions. Thus, if you choose to forget the "Experimental researches" and remember only the Calvinistic sermons, you can say of Faraday that he was much less a man of science than a nonconformist preacher. Concentrate on Clerk Maxwell's beautiful letters, and you will be able to conclude that the author of the electromagnetic theory of light was not so much the successor of Newton as of Mme. de Sévigné and Horace Walpole. And if you listen to the musical improvisations rather than to the lectures on relativity, you will have every reason for saying that Einstein is more significant as a violinist than as a mathematical physicist.

Such conclusions are based, as I have said, on systematic and selective ignorance. Now, systematic ignorance of past science is doubtless deplorable. But, however deplorable, it is not, except with a special effort, to be avoided. Those who have not had a scientific education are incapable of understanding the technicalities of any scientific paper. Those who have been educated in one branch of science are hardly better off than laymen, when it comes to understanding a paper in some other branch. And those who have been educated in the particular science under consideration have no need to refer to the original papers of their predecessors. Every generation of scientific men starts where the previous generation left off; and the most advanced discoveries of one age constitute the elementary axioms of the next. We are not in the habit of inspecting the foundations of the houses in which we live; and, similarly, men of science are not in the habit of referring to the original paper of their predecessors. "I am toiling over my chapter about Owen," writes Huxley towards the end of his life, in 1894. "The thing that strikes me most is, how he and I and all the things we fought about belong to antiquity." It was, to a large extent, thanks to Huxley's own labours that they belonged to antiquity. A prolific discoverer is continuously superannuating his earlier self.

Except, then, for the historians of science, nobody studies at first hand those contributions to knowledge to which the great discoverers of the past owe their scientific reputations. By what seems a strange paradox, the older scientists survive mainly as artists. A work of art can never be taken for granted, and so forgotten; neither can it ever be disproved and therefore thrown aside. Science is soon out of date, art is not.

Of this fact Huxley himself was well aware. In one of his letters he comments upon it with characteristic humour. "At the Christmas dinner," we are told in his biography, "he invariably delighted the children by carving wonderful beasts, generally pigs, out of orange peel. When the marriage of his eldest daughter had taken her away from this important function, she was sent the best specimen as a reminder. 'I call it,' he writes in the accompanying letter, 'Piggurne, or Harmony in Orange and White.'" This was written in 1878, the year of Whistler's action against Ruskin; nocturnes and colour harmonies were very much "in the news." "'Preserve it, my dear child,' he goes on, 'as evidence of the paternal genius, when those light and fugitive productions which are buried in the *Philosophical Transactions* and elsewhere are forgotten.'"

The jesting words express a truth. Productions published in the *Philosophical Transactions* of the Royal Society may not be light; but they are in a very real sense fugitive. The substance of a scientific paper is incorporated into the general stock of knowledge; but the paper itself is doomed to oblivion. Not so the pig made of orange peel. If sufficiently well carved, it may continue to give pleasure and to excite admiration for an indefinite period—or at any rate so long as the peel holds together. What is true of orange-peel pigs is true, *a fortiori,* of those monuments more lasting than brass, well-written books.

As a scientific man, Huxley, like all his great contemporaries and predecessors, is now a mere historical figure. Most of us are content to accept his scientific reputation on authority, without ever having consulted the original evidence on which it was based. As a literary man, however, he is still a living force. His non-technical writings have the persistent contemporariness that is a quality of all good art. People go on reading his books and enjoying them. Mr. Chesterton affirms, as a matter of historical fact, that Huxley "was much more of a literary than a scientific man." In which Mr. Chesterton is wrong. But if he had said that Huxley "*is* much more of a literary than a scientific man," he would have been quite right. In so far as Huxley is still alive, influential and contemporary, it is as the man of letters. Such is the privilege of art. Orange-peel pigs are less transient than scientific papers.

There are several ways in which I might deal with Huxley's career as a man of letters. There is, for example, the biographical approach. But the biographical ground has been so thoroughly covered in the *Life and Letters* that I could do nothing in this line but summarize what has been said before. I prefer, therefore, to approach the subject as a purely literary critic. Now, much has been written in rather vague and general terms of Huxley's style. I shall, accordingly, try to do something more definite and precise. Taking characteristic specimens of Huxley's writings, I shall analyse them with a view to showing what exactly were the technical means he employed to produce his effects. Critics, it seems to me, content themselves too often with the mere application of epithets. Majestic, flat, sublime, passionate—criticism is in many cases just a calling of laudatory or disparaging names. But this is not enough. Critics should take pains to show why such and such a piece of writing provokes us to call it by such and such a name. The observable facts of literature are words arranged in certain patterns. The words have a meaning independent of the pattern in which they are arranged; but it is the pattern that gives to this meaning its peculiar quality and intensity; that can make a statement seem somehow truer or somehow less true than the truth. Moreover, a word-pattern of one kind will cause us to say of its inventor: "This man is (for example) sincere"; of another kind: "This man is affected and false." It is the business of the literary artist to make word-patterns in such a way that his readers shall be compelled to draw certain inferences from them. It is the business of the critic to show how our judgments are affected by variations in word-patterns. This is what I shall try to do in the present case.

But before beginning my analysis of Huxley's

achievements as a literary artist, I think it would be advisable to say a few words by way of general introduction about the relations between literature and science.

The function of language is twofold: to communicate emotion and to give information. The rudimentary language of the lower animals seems to be purely emotive. Beasts make noises to express desire, fear, anger and the like; to let off their superfluous energy; and to make their presence known to their fellow-creatures. Never do they express a concept. When a startled blackbird flies off at our approach with his characteristic cry, he is not saying, "There is a man"; he is saying, "I am afraid"—or rather, he is simply screaming with terror. And at the sound of the scream, other blackbirds are terrified. Communication is by emotional infection, never, apparently, by conceptual statement.

Man has invented concepts. He does not merely scream with terror: he also says why and of what he is afraid. The noises he makes stand for classes of objects. He can do what the animal can never do: he can make an exact statement untinged by passion. In other words, he can write scientifically.

But because he *can* do this, it does not follow that he very often wants to do it. In most of the circumstances of life, he wants not only to inform, but also to move—above all, to be moved as well as to be in-

[53]

formed. Literature is the art of making statements movingly.

Now, the emotions which a literary statement may cause us to feel are of two distinct types. They may be what I will call the "biological emotions"—emotions, that is to say, with a survival value, such as fear, anger, delight or disgust, all of which we share with the lower animals. Or they may be more specifically human emotions—luxury feelings, which we might lose without seriously imperilling our chances of survival.

Literature, in common with the other arts, arouses in us, over and above any kind of biological emotion, a certain luxury feeling, to which we give the name of the aesthetic emotion. We describe as beautiful anything which makes us experience this feeling.

Let us now consider the case of a writer who is trying to make a statement which shall cause his readers to have a certain biological feeling—say, a feeling of anger. By using words with suitable significances and associations, by expressing himself in terms of metaphors that call up the right kind of images, he can make it clear to his readers that he feels angry himself (or, vicariously, in the person of a fictional character) and that he wants them to feel angry too. Whether they respond or remain unmoved depends, to a very considerable extent, on his powers as an artist—on his powers, that is to say, as a giver of aesthetic emotions. If he can arrange his words and phrases in a pattern which his readers will consider beautiful, then he is likely to succeed. If not, he is likely to fail. Biological feelings can be well and promptly communicated only by words arranged so as to give us aesthetic feelings. And the same thing is true even of the most abstract ideas. We are more likely to take in an idea which is expressed with art, beautifully, than if it is expressed in language that gives us no aesthetic satisfaction.

True, facts and theories *can* be communicated in terms that give the reader no aesthetic satisfaction. So can the passions. But neither passion nor facts and theories can be communicated rapidly and persuasively in such terms. Whatever is expressed with art—whether it be a lover's despair or a metaphysical theory—pierces the mind and compels assent and acceptance. Against that which is expressed without art, our understandings are naturally armoured. We have a certain difficulty in taking in anything that is not intrinsically elegant; a certain eagerness to accept anything that moves us aesthetically. Handsome faces are sometimes associated with ugly characters; and in the same way, alas! literary art may be associated with untruth. The natural human tendency to believe what is beautiful has been the source of innumerable errors. If only Plato had written as badly as Immanuel Kant! But his voice was, unfortunately, the voice of an angel, even when it was uttering demonstrable nonsense. And if Darwin's style had been as excellent as Samuel Butler's, Mr. Bernard Shaw

[55]

would not at present be a preacher of Lamarckism—
"a doctrine," as Professor J. B. S. Haldane has remarked, "supported by far less positive evidence than
exists for the reality of witchcraft."

Science is investigation. But if it were only investigation, it would be without fruit, and useless. Henry
Cavendish investigated for the mere fun of the thing,
and left the world in ignorance of his most important
discoveries. Our admiration for his genius is tempered
by a certain disapproval; we feel that such a man is
selfish and anti-social. Science is investigation; yes. But
it is also, and no less essentially, communication. But
all communication is literature. In one of its aspects,
then, science is a branch of literature.

It may be objected that I apply the term "literature"
too indiscriminately—that, instead of using the word
to cover all verbal communications whatsoever, I
should limit its connotation to a certain class of communications. To this objection, I reply interrogatively:
Which particular class of verbal communications constitutes literature? The answers to this question are
generally very vague. For example, literature has been
defined as "the interpretation of life through the medium of words"; while a distinction is often drawn
between "words used to record observations of fact,
either as an end in themselves, or as a basis for generalizations, and words used as a means for transferring
experience." But, frankly, this sort of thing won't do;

it is too hazy. Not much better is the distinction between literature and science implied by Wordsworth
in his preface to the *Lyrical Ballads.* "The remotest discoveries of the chemist, the botanist, or the mineralogist
will be as proper objects of the poet's art as any upon
which he is now employed, if the time should ever
come, when these things shall be familiar to us, and the
relations under which they are contemplated shall be
manifestly and palpably material to us as enjoying and
suffering beings." But who, we may inquire, are the
people whom Wordsworth calls "us"? Is it not obvious
that the more intelligent a man is, and the more highly
cultivated, the wider will be the range of things which
are "material to him as an enjoying and suffering
being"? Moreover, as every verbal communication can
be made well or badly, every verbal communication is
susceptible of affecting some men, at any rate, as
aesthetic enjoyers and sufferers. It goes without saying,
of course, that only those who understand the terms in
which the communication is made will have any
aesthetic feelings about it. Englishmen are clearly not
the best judges of Chinese poetry, and those who have
not had a scientific education will be unable to understand, much less to appreciate and enjoy, works written
in a highly technical language. But for anyone who
knows what he is talking about, the very mathematicians are men of letters—men of algebraical letters,
no doubt; but even x and *sigma* and *psi* can be aestheti-

cally good or bad, *litterae humaniores* or inhuman letters. I have heard mathematicians groaning over the demonstrations of Kelvin. Ponderous and clumsy, they bludgeon the mind into a reluctant assent. Whereas to be convinced by Clerk Maxwell's elegant equations is a pleasure; and reading Niels Abel on hyperelliptic functions is almost, it seems, like listening to Mozart's chamber music. For the mathematically illiterate, like myself, these things are, of course, mere scribblings, without significance and without form. For those whom Nature has endowed with suitable talents and who have had the right education, they are works of art, some exquisite, some atrociously bad. What is true of a mathematical argument is equally true of arguments couched in words. Even plain records of observed fact may be, in their own way, beautiful or ugly. From all of which we must conclude that all verbal communications whatsoever are literature.

Some kinds of literature, however, are more widely accessible than others. Also, certain classes of experience give more artistic scope to those who communicate them than do certain other classes of experience. For example, a man who writes about his experiences of love or pain has more scope for arranging words in an aesthetically satisfying way than one who sets out to give an account of his observations on, say, deep-sea fish. All communications are literature; but their potentialities for beauty are unequal. A good account of deep-sea fish can never be as richly, variously and subtly beautiful as a good poem about love. But, on the other hand, a bad account of fish can probably never be so monstrous as a bad love-poem.

To make clearer what I have been saying, let me give two specific examples. The following is an extract from an article in the *Encyclopaedia Britannica* on the furnishing of Anglican churches after the Reformation: "When tables were substituted for altars in the English churches, these were not merely movable, but, at the administration of the Lord's Supper, were actually moved into the body of the church, and placed *table-wise*—that is, with the long sides turned to the north and south, and the narrow ends to the east and west. In the time of Archbishop Laud, however, the present practice of the Church of England was introduced. The communion table, though still of wood and movable, is, in fact, never moved; it is placed *altar-wise*—that is, with the longer axis running north and south. Often there is a reredos behind it; it is also fenced in by rails to preserve it from profanation of various kinds."

This is a simple and, as it happens, not a very good specimen of scientific literature. We read it without feeling any emotion, whether biological or aesthetic. The words are neither exciting nor beautiful; they are merely informative—and informative in what is, on the whole, rather an inelegant way.

Let us now listen to what Milton had to say on the

same subject. "The table of communion, now become a table of separation, stands like an exalted platform on the brow of the quire, fortified with bulwark and barricado to keep off the profane touch of the laics, whilst the obscene and surfeited priest scruples not to paw and mammock the sacramental bread as familiarly as his tavern biscuit."

This is a statement about church furnishing; but not, as I think you may have noticed, a scientific statement —that is to say, a merely informative and unimpassioned statement. Milton, it is clear, designed to communicate, along with the facts about altars, certain biological feelings of his own—as hatred of priests and sympathy for an exploited laity. Thanks to the skilful use of a number of technical literary devices—devices which, unfortunately, I have no time to describe and analyse—the passage also gives us a lively feeling of aesthetic satisfaction. Milton communicates what he has to say with art; that is to say, he communicates it successfully. He really makes us feel, at any rate while we are reading him, some of his own indignation.

Huxley, as I shall show in due course, was an artist in both these kinds of literature—an artist in pure scientific statement, and also, on occasion, an artist in the communication of what I have called the biological feelings. Both his pure scientific and his emotive statements arouse aesthetic feelings; in other words, each kind of statement is, in its own way, beautiful.

Huxley realized very well the importance of being an artist. Of the Germans he writes: "As men of research in positive science they are magnificently laborious and accurate. But most of them have no notion of style, and seem to compose their books with a pitchfork." Determined that his own books should not justify a similar reproach, he cultivated his literary gifts with conscientious industry. "It constantly becomes more and more difficult for me to *finish* things satisfactorily," he writes to Hooker in 1860. The reason for this was that his standard of literary excellence was constantly becoming higher. Let me quote in this context a letter to his French translator, de Varigny. "I am quite conscious that the condensed and idiomatic English into which I always try to put my thoughts must present many difficulties to a translator. . . . The fact is that I have a great love and respect for my native tongue, and take great pains to use it properly. Sometimes I write essays half a dozen times before I can get them into the proper shape; and I believe I become more fastidious as I grow older." It was an effective fastidiousness; Huxley undoubtedly wrote better as he grew older.

What were his artistic principles and ideals? The following passage from a letter to the *Pall Mall Gazette* in 1886 is illuminating:

That a young Englishman may be turned out of one of our universities, "epopt and perfect," as far as their system takes him, and yet ignorant of the noble literature which

[61]

has grown up in these islands during the last three centuries, no less than of the philosophical and political ideas which have most profoundly influenced modern civilization, is a fact in the history of the nineteenth century which the twentieth will find hard to believe; though perhaps it is not more incredible than our current superstition that whoso wishes to write and speak English well should mould his style after the models furnished by classical antiquity. For my part, I venture to doubt the wisdom of attempting to mould one's style by any other process than that of striving after the clear and forcible expression of definite conceptions; in which process the Glassian precept, "first catch your definite conceptions," is probably the most difficult to obey. But still I mark among distinguished contemporary speakers and writers of English, saturated with antiquity, not a few to whom, it seems to me, the study of Hobbes might have taught dignity, of Swift, concision and clearness, of Goldsmith and Defoe, simplicity.

Well, among a hundred young men whose university career is finished, is there one whose attention has ever been directed by his literary instructors to a page of Hobbes, or Swift, or Goldsmith, or Defoe? In my boyhood we were familiar with *Robinson Crusoe, The Vicar of Wakefield* and *Gulliver's Travels;* and though the treasures of "Middle English" were hidden from us, my impression is that we ran less chance of learning to write and speak the "middling English" of popular orators and head masters than if we had been perfect in such mysteries and ignorant of those three masterpieces. It has been the fashion to decry the eighteenth century, as young fops laugh at their fathers. But we were there in germ; and a "Professor of Eighteenth-Century History and Literature" who knew his business might tell young Englishmen more of that which it is profoundly important that they should know, but which at present remains hidden from them, than any other instructor: and, incidentally, they would learn to know good English when they see or hear it—perhaps even to distinguish between slipshod copiousness and true eloquence, and that alone would be a great gain.

To literary beginners, Huxley's advice was: "Say that which has to be said in such language that you can stand cross-examination on each word." And again: "Be clear, though you may be convicted of error. If you are clearly wrong, you will run up against a fact sometime and get set right. If you shuffle with your subject and study chiefly to use language which will give you a loophole of escape either way, there is no hope for you." "Veracity," he said on another occasion, "is the heart of morality." It was also the heart of his literary style. For all those rhetorical devices by means of which the sophist and the politician seek to make the worse appear the better cause Huxley felt an almost passionate disapproval. "When some chieftain," he wrote, "famous in political warfare, ventures into the region of letters or of science, in full confidence that the methods which have brought fame and honour in his own province will answer there, he is apt to forget that he will be judged by those people on whom rhetorical artifices have long since ceased to take effect; and to whom mere dexterity in putting together cleverly ambiguous

[63]

phrases, and even the great art of offensive misrepresentation, are unspeakably wearisome."

The chieftain in question was Mr. Gladstone, with whom, in 1891, Huxley was having the Gadarene swine controversy. Four years later, in the last year of his life, Huxley was to remark, in a conversation recorded by Mr. Wilfrid Ward, on the philosophical methods of another eminent politician, Mr. Arthur Balfour. "No human being holds the opinion he (Balfour) speaks of as Naturalism. He is a good debater. He knows the value of a word. The word 'Naturalism' has a bad sound and unpleasant associations. It would tell against us in the House of Commons, and so it will with his readers." Huxley was also a good debater; he also knew the value of a word. But his passion for veracity always kept him from taking any unfair rhetorical advantages of an opponent. The candour with which he acknowledged a weakness in his own case was always complete, and though he made full use of a rich variety of literary devices to bring home what he wanted to say, he never abused his great rhetorical powers. Truth was more important to him than personal triumph, and he relied more on a forceful clarity to convince his readers than on the brilliant and exciting ambiguities of propagandist eloquence.

For the purposes of literary analysis, Huxley's writings may be divided into three classes: first, the purely descriptive; secondly, the philosophical and sociological; and thirdly, the controversial and (to use once more a repellant, but irreplaceable, word) the emotive. To the first of these classes belong the technical scientific papers; to the second, the studies of Hume and Berkeley and a number of essays on metaphysical, ethical and educational subjects; and to the third, certain of the essays on Christian and Hebrew tradition and the essays containing criticisms of other people's ideas or a defence of his own. It is hardly necessary to say that, in reality, the three classes overlap. The descriptive papers contain philosophical matter in the form of generalizations and scientific hypotheses. The philosophical and sociological essays have their controversial and their emotionally moving passages; and as most of the controversies are on philosophical subjects, the controversial essays are to a considerable extent purely philosophical. Still, imperfect as it is, the classification is none the less useful. The writings of the first two classes are strictly scientific writings; that is to say, they are meant to communicate facts and ideas, not passions. They are of the same kind as the passage from the *Encyclopaedia* quoted at an earlier stage in this lecture. The writings of the third class belong to the same genus as my quotation from Milton. They are intended to communicate feelings as well as information—and biological feeling as well as pure aesthetic feeling. I propose now to deal with these three classes of Huxley's writings in order.

[65]

To describe with precision even the simplest object is extremely difficult. Just how difficult only those who have attempted the task professionally can realize. Let me ask you to imagine yourselves suddenly called upon to explain to some Martian visitor the exact form, function and mode of operation of, say, a corkscrew. The thing seems simple enough; and yet I suspect that, after a few minutes of stammering hesitations, most of us would find ourselves reduced to making spiral gestures with a forefinger and going through a pantomime of bottle-opening. The difficulties of describing in a clear and intelligible way such an incomparably more elaborate piece of machinery as a living organism, for example, are proportionately greater.

Not only is exact description difficult; it is also, of all kinds of writing, that which has in it the least potentialities of beauty. The object to be described stares the author uncompromisingly in the face. His business is to render its likeness in words, point by point, in such a way that someone who had never seen it would be able to reconstruct it from his description, as from a blue print. He must therefore call every spade consistently and exclusively a spade—never anything else. But the higher forms of literature depend for many of their most delicate effects on spades being called on occasion by other names. Non-scientific writers are free to use a variety of synonyms to express the same idea in subtly different ways; are free to em-

ploy words with variously coloured overtones of association; are free to express themselves, in terms now of
one metaphor, now of another. Not so the maker of
verbal blue prints. The only beauties he can hope, or,
indeed, has any right to create are beauties of orderly
composition and, in detail, of verbal clarity. Huxley's
scientific papers prove him to have had a remarkable
talent for this austere and ungrateful kind of writing.
His descriptions of the most complicated organic struc-
tures are astonishingly lucid. We are reminded, as we
read, that their author was an accomplished draughts-
man. "I should make it absolutely necessary," he writes
in one of his essays on education, "for everybody to
learn to draw. . . . You will find it," he goes on, "an
implement of learning of extreme value. It gives you
the means of training the young in attention and accuracy, which are two things in which all mankind are
more deficient than in any other mental quality whatever. The whole of my life has been spent in trying
to give my proper attention to things and to be accurate, and I have not succeeded as well as I could wish;
and other people, I am afraid, are not much more
fortunate." No artist, I suppose, has ever succeeded as
well as he could wish; but many have succeeded as
well as other, less talented people could wish. In its
own kind, such a book as Huxley's Treatise on the
Crayfish is a model of excellence. Quotation cannot do
justice to the composition of the book as a whole, and

the unavoidable use of technical terms makes the citing even of short extracts unsuitable on such an occasion as the present. The following passage may serve, however, to give some idea of the lucidity of Huxley's descriptive style:

In the dorsal wall of the heart two small oval apertures are visible, provided with valvular lips, which open inwards, or towards the internal cavity of the heart. There is a similar aperture in each of the two lateral faces of the heart, and two others in its inferior face, making six in all. These apertures readily admit fluid into the heart, but oppose its exit. On the other hand, at the origins of the arteries there are small valvular folds directed in such a manner as to permit the exit of fluid from the heart, while they prevent its entrance.

This is nakedly plain and unadorned; but it does what it was intended to do—gives the reader a satisfyingly accurate picture of what is being described. Some modern popularizers of science have sought to "humanize" their writing. The following is an example of the late Dr. Dorsey's humanized—his all-too-humanized—scientific style:

If we find that the thing we trust to pick the mother of our childrn is simply a double-barrelled pump, knowledge of our heart or the liquid refreshment it pumps to our brains will not grow more nerve cells, but it should make us less nervous and more respectful of the pump and the refreshment it delivers; when it stops, the brain starves to death.

[68]

Obscure almost to meaninglessness, vulgar, vague—this is the humanization of science with a vengeance! Deplorably but, I suppose, naturally enough, this kind of popular science is thoroughly popular in the other, the box-office sense of the term. Tennyson's generalization, that we needs must love the highest when we see it, has but the slenderest justification in observable fact.

So much for the writings of the first class. Those of the second are more interesting, both to the general reader and to the literary critic. Philosophical writings have much higher potentialities of beauty than purely descriptive writings. The descriptive writer is confined within the narrow prison of the material objects whose likeness he is trying to render. The philosopher is the inhabitant of a much more spacious, because a purely mental, universe. There is, if I may so express myself, more room in the theory of knowledge than in a crayfish's heart. No doubt, if we could feel as certain about epistemology as we do about the shape and function of crustacean viscera, the philosopher's universe would be as narrow as the descriptive naturalist's. But we do not feel as certain. Ignorance has many advantages. Man's uncertainties in regard to all the major issues of life allow the philosopher much enviable freedom—freedom, among other things, to employ all kinds of artistic devices, from the use of which the descriptive naturalist is quite debarred.

The passages from Huxley's philosophical writings

which I now propose to quote and analyse have been chosen mainly, of course, because they exhibit characteristic excellences of style, but partly, also, for the sake of their content. Huxley's philosophical doctrines are outside my province, and I shall not discuss them. What I have done, however, is to choose as my literary examples passages which illustrate his views on a number of important questions. They show how cautious and profound a thinker he was—how very far from being that arrogant and cocksure materialist at whom, as at a convenient Aunt Sally, certain contemporary publicists are wont to fling their dialectical brickbats.

Huxley's use of purely rhythmical effects was always masterly, and my first three examples are intended to illustrate his practice in this branch of literary art. Here is a paragraph on scientific hypotheses:

All science starts with hypotheses—in other words, with assumptions that are unproved, while they may be, and often are, erroneous, but which are better than nothing to the searcher after order in the maze of phenomena. And the historical progress of every science depends on the criticism of hypotheses—on the gradual stripping off, that is, of their untrue or superfluous parts—until there remains only that exact verbal expression of as much as we know of the facts, and no more, which constitutes a perfect scientific theory.

The substance of this paragraph happens to be intrinsically correct. But we are the more willing to believe its truth because of the way in which that truth is expressed. Huxley's utterance has something peculiarly judicious and persuasive about it. The secret is to be found in his rhythm. If we analyse the crucial first sentence, we shall find that it consists of three more or less equal long phrases, followed by three more or less equal short ones. Thus:

> All science starts with hypotheses—
> in other words, with assumptions that are unproved,
> while they may be, and often are, erroneous;
> but which are better than nothing
> to the searcher after order
> in the maze of phenomena.

The long opening phrases state all that can be said against hypotheses—state it with a firm and heavy emphasis. Then, suddenly, in the second half of the sentence, the movement quickens, and the brisk and lively rhythm of the three last phrases brings home the value of hypotheses with an appeal to the aesthetic sensibilities as well as to the intellect.

My second example is from a passage dealing with "those who oppose the doctrine of necessity":

> They rest [writes Huxley] on the absurd presumption that the proposition "I can do as I like" is contradictory to the doctrine of necessity. The answer is: nobody doubts that, at any rate within certain limits, you can do as you like. But what determines your likings and dislikings? Did you make your own constitution? Is it your contrivance that one thing is pleasant and another is painful? And even if it were, why did you prefer to make it after the one

fashion rather than the other? The passionate assertion of the consciousness of their freedom, which is the favorite refuge of the opponents of the doctrine of necessity, is mere futility for nobody denies it. What they really have to do, if they would upset the necessarian argument, is to prove that they are free to associate any emotion whatever with any idea whatever; to like pain as much as pleasure, vice as much as virtue; in short, to prove that, whatever may be the fixity of order of the universe of things, that of thought is given over to chance.

Again, this is a very sound argument; but its penetrative force and immediate persuasiveness are unquestionably increased by the manner of its expression. The anti-necessarian case is attacked in a series of short, sharp phrases, each carrying a simple question demanding a simple and, for the arguer's opponents, a most damaging answer:

But what determines your likings and dislikings?
Did you make your own constitution?
Is it your contrivance that one thing is pleasant and another is painful?

The phrases lengthen as the argument deals with subtler points of detail; then, in the last sentence, where Huxley convicts his opponents of upholding an absurdity, they contract to the emphatically alliterative brevity of

to like pain as much as pleasure,
vice as much as virtue.

[72]

After which the absurdity of the anti-necessarian case is generalized; there is a long preparatory phrase, followed by a brief, simple and, we are made to feel, definitive conclusion:

to prove that, whatever may be the fixity of order of the universe of things,
that of thought is given over to chance.

The persuasive effectiveness of these last phrases is enhanced by the use of alliteration. "Things" and "thought" are key words. Their alliterative resemblance serves to emphasize the unjustifiable distinction which the anti-necessarians draw between the two worlds. And the insistent recurrence in both phrases of the v-sound of *prove, whatever, universe* and of *given* and *over* enhances the same effect.

The passage I am now about to quote is remarkable both for what it says and for the particularly solemn and noble manner of the saying:

In whichever way we look at the matter, morality is based on feeling, not on reason; though reason alone is competent to trace out the effects of our actions and thereby dictate conduct. Justice is founded on the love of one's neighbour; and goodness is a kind of beauty. The moral law, like the laws of physical nature, rests in the long run upon instinctive intuitions, and is neither more nor less "innate" and "necessary" than they are. Some people cannot by any means be got to understand the first book of Euclid; but the truths of mathematics are no less necessary and binding on the great mass of mankind. Some there

[73]

are who cannot feel the difference between the "Sonata
Appassionate" and "Cherry Ripe," or between a grave-
stone-cutter's cherub and the Apollo Belvedere; but the
canons of art are none the less acknowledged. While some
there may be who, devoid of sympathy, are incapable of a
sense of duty; but neither does their existence affect the
foundations of morality. Such pathological deviations from
true manhood are merely the halt, the lame and the blind
of the world of consciousness; and the anatomist of the
mind leaves them aside, as the anatomist of the body would
ignore abnormal specimens.

And as there are Pascals and Mozarts, Newtons and
Raphaels, in which the innate faculty for science or art
needs but a touch to spring into full vigour, and through
whom the human race obtains new possibilities of knowledge and new conceptions of beauty; so there have been
men of moral genius, to whom we owe ideals of duty and
visions of moral perfection, which ordinary mankind could
never have attained; though, happily for them, they can
feel the beauty of a vision which lay beyond the reach of
their dull imaginations, and count life well spent in shap-
ing some faint image of it in the actual world.

As a piece of reflective writing, this is quite admirable; and it will be worth while, I think, to take some
trouble to analyse out the technical devices which make
it so effective. The secret of the peculiar beauty of this
grave and noble passage is to be found, I believe, in the
author's use of what, for lack of a better term, I will
call "caesura-sentences." Hebrew literature provides the
classical type of the caesura-sentence. Open any of the
poetical books of the Bible at random, and you will

find all the examples you want. "His soul shall dwell at ease; and his seed shall inherit the earth." Or, "Then shall the dust return to the earth as it was; and the spirit shall return unto God who gave it." The whole system of Hebrew poetry was based on the division of each sentence by a caesura into two distinct, but related clauses. Anglo-Saxon verse was written on a somewhat similar principle. The caesura-sentence is common in the work of some of the greatest English prose-writers. One of them, Sir Thomas Browne, used it constantly. Here, for example, is a characteristic passage from the "Urn Burial": "Darkness and light divide the course of time, and oblivion shares with memory a great part even of our living beings. We slightly remember our felicities, and the smartest strokes of affliction leave but short smart upon us. Sense endureth no extremities, and sorrows destroy us or themselves." It was Browne, I think, who first demonstrated the peculiar suitability of the caesura-sentence for the expression of grave meditations on the nature of things, for the utterance of profound and rather melancholy aphorisms. The clauses into which he divides his sentence are generally short. Sometimes the two clauses are more or less evenly balanced. Sometimes a longer clause is succeeded by a shorter, and the effect is one of finality, of the last word having been spoken. Sometimes the shorter comes first, and the long clause after the caesura seems to open

[75]

up wide prospects of contemplation and speculative argument.

I could give other examples of the use of caesura-sentences by writers as far apart as Dr. Johnson and De Quincey. But time presses; and besides, these examples would be superfluous. For, as it so happens, Huxley's use of the caesura-sentence is very similar to Browne's. He employs it, in the great majority of cases, when he wants to express himself in meditative aphorisms about the nature of life in general. Thus: "Ignorance is visited as sharply as wilful disobedience—incapacity meets with the same punishment as crime." Again, "Pain and sorrow knock at our doors more loudly than pleasure and happiness; and the prints of their heavy footsteps are less easily effaced." Here is another example, where the clauses are much shorter: "There is but one right, and the possibilities of wrong are infinite." Here yet one more, in which, as the statement made is more complicated, the clauses have to be longer than usual: "It is one of the last lessons one learns from experience, but not the least important, that a heavy tax is levied upon all forms of success; and that failure is one of the commonest disguises assumed by blessings."

In the long passage quoted just now much of that effect of noble and meditative gravity is obtained by the judicious use of caesura-sentences. The tone is set by a sentence that might almost have been penned by

[76]

Sir Thomas Browne himself: "Justice is founded on the love of one's neighbour; and goodness is a kind of beauty." All the rest of the first paragraph is built up of fundamentally similar caesura-sentences, some almost as brief and simple as the foregoing, some long and complicated, but preserving through their length and complication the peculiar quality (as of a sad and deeply reflective soliloquy, an argument of the mind with its inmost self), the musically pensive essence of the Brownean formula.

Before leaving the subject of Huxley's philosophical writings, I must say something about his use of images and his choice of words. Since accuracy and veracity were the qualities at which he consistently aimed, Huxley was sparing in the use of images. Ideas can be very vividly expressed in terms of metaphor and simile; but, since analogies are rarely complete, this vividness is too often achieved at the cost of precision. Seldom, and only with the greatest caution, does Huxley attempt anything like a full-blown simile. The most striking one I can remember is that in which he compares living beings to the whirlpool below Niagara:

However changeful is the contour of its crest, this wave has been visible, approximately in the same place, and with the same general form, for centuries past. Seen from a mile off, it would seem to be a stationary hillock of water. Viewed closely, it is a typical expression of the conflicting impulses generated by a swift rush of material particles.

Now, with all our appliances, we cannot get within a good many miles, so to speak, of the crayfish. If we could, we should see that it was nothing but the constant form of a similar turmoil of material molecules, which are constantly flowing into the animal on one side, and streaming out on the other.

Only where analogies were as close as this one between the living body and the vortex would Huxley venture to make use of similes. He was never prepared to enliven the manner of his books at the expense of their matter.

Huxley's vocabulary is probably the weakest point in all his literary equipment. True, it was perfectly adequate to the clear and forceful statement of his ideas. But the sensitive reader cannot help feeling that the choice of words might, without any impairment of scientific efficiency, have been more exquisite. For example, we miss in his writings that studied alternation of words of Greek and Latin with words of Teutonic origin—an alternation so rich, when skilfully handled, as by Milton, in powerful and startling literary effects. To illustrate the defects in Huxley's vocabulary would be a lengthy and laborious process, which I cannot undertake in the time at my disposal. It must be enough to say that, good as his choice of words generally is, it might unquestionably have been better.

Let us turn now to the third division of Huxley's writings, the controversial and emotive. As a controversialist, Huxley was severe, but always courteous. We must not expect to find in his polemical writings those thunderous comminations, that jeering and abuse which make Milton's prose such lively reading. Still, he could be sarcastic enough when he wanted, and his wit was pointed and barbed by the elegance with which he expressed himself. Here is a passage from a brief biography of Descartes, which shows what was the nature of his talents in this direction:

Trained by the best educators of the seventeenth century, the Jesuits; naturally endowed with a dialectic grasp and subtlety which even they could hardly improve; and with a passion for getting at the truth which even they could hardly impair, Descartes possessed in addition a rare mastery of literary expression.

One could quote many similar passages. From the neat antithesis to the odd and laughter-provoking word —Huxley used every device for the expression of sarcasm and irony.

In the passages in which his aim was to convey, along with ideas, a certain quality of passion, Huxley resorted very often to literary allusion—particularly to biblical allusion. Here is a characteristic example:

The politician tells us, "You must educate the masses because they are going to be masters." The clergy join in the cry for education, for they affirm that the people are drifting away from church and chapel into the broadest infidelity. The manufacturers and the capitalists swell the chorus lustily. They declare that ignorance makes bad

[79]

workmen; that England will soon be unable to turn out cotton goods, or steam engines, cheaper than other people; and then, Ichabod! Ichabod! the glory will be departed from us. And a few voices are lifted up in favour of the doctrine that the masses should be educated because they are men and women with unlimited capacities of being, doing and suffering, and that it is as true now as ever it was, that the people perish for lack of knowledge.

Here the two, or rather the three, biblical references produce a variety of powerful emotional effects—produce them, let us note in passing, only upon those who know their Bible. Those who do not know their Bible will fail to appreciate the chief beauties of this passage almost as completely as those who do not know their Functions of Complex Variables must fail to appreciate the beauties of Niels Abel's mathematical literature. Every writer assumes in his readers a knowledge of the work of certain other writers. His assumptions, I may add, are frequently quite unjustified.

Let us now consider the emotional effects which Huxley aimed at producing and which, upon those who know the sacred writings as well as he, he did and still does produce. Ichabod, it will be remembered, was so named, "because the glory is departed from Israel, for the ark of God is taken." To mention Ichabod in this context is to imply a richly sarcastic disquisition on the nature of the capitalists' god. The tone changes, in the last sentence, from ironical to earnest and pathetic;

and those final words, "the people perish for lack of knowledge," put us in mind of two noble biblical passages: one from the book of the prophet Hosea, who affirms that "the Lord hath a controversy with the inhabitants of the land" and that "the people are destroyed for lack of knowledge"; the other from the book of Proverbs, to the effect that "where there is no vision, the people perish." The double reference produces the effect Huxley desired. The true reason for universal education could not be stated more concisely or more movingly.

Occasionally, Huxley's biblical references take the form, not of direct citation, but of the use of little tags of obsolescent language borrowed from the Authorized Version. After a long passage of lucid and essentially modern exposition, he will sometimes announce the oncoming of his peroration by a phrase or two of sixteenth-century prayer-book or Bible English. Our modern taste has veered away from this practice; but among writers of the early and middle nineteenth century it was very common. Lamb and his contemporaries were constantly dropping into Wardour Street Elizabethan; Carlyle's writings are a warehouse of every kind of fancy-dress language; Herman Melville made a habit of breaking out, whenever he was excited, into bogus Shakespeare; the very love-letters of the Brownings are peppered with learned archaisms. Indeed, one of the major defects of nineteenth-century literature, at any rate in our eyes, was its inordinate literariness, its habit of verbal dressing up and playing stylistic charades. That Huxley should have made brief and occasional use of the literary devices so freely exploited by his contemporaries is not surprising. Fortunately, his passion for veracity prevented him from overdoing the literariness.

I have constantly spoken, in the course of these analyses, of "literary devices." The phrase is a rather unfortunate one; for it is liable to call up in the hearer's mind a picture of someone laboriously practising a mixture of card-sharping and cookery. The words make us visualize the man of letters turning over the pages of some literary Mrs. Beeton in quest of the best recipe for an epigram or a dirge; or else as a trickster preparing for his game with the reader by carefully marking the cards. But in point of fact the man of letters does most of his work not by calculation, not by the application of formulas, but by aesthetic intuition. He has something to say, and he sets it down in the words which he finds most satisfying aesthetically. After the event comes the critic, who discovers that he was using a certain kind of literary device, which can be classified in its proper chapter of the cookery-book. The process is largely irreversible. Lacking talent, you cannot, out of the cookery-book, concoct a good work of art. The best you can hope to do is to produce an imitation, which may, for a short time, deceive the unwary into thinking it the genuine article.

Huxley's was unquestionably the genuine article. In this necessarily perfunctory discussion of a few characteristic examples of his writing, I have tried to show why he was a great man of letters, and how he produced those artistic effects, which cause us to make this critical judgment. The analysis might be carried much further, but not by a lecturer and not within the lecturer's allotted hour. "Had we but world enough and time . . ." Alas! we never have.

Words and Behaviour

WORDS form the thread on which we string our experiences. Without them we should live spasmodically and intermittently. Hatred itself is not so strong that animals will not forget it, if distracted, even in the presence of the enemy. Watch a pair of cats, crouching on the brink of a fight. Balefully the eyes glare; from far down in the throat of each come bursts of a strange, strangled noise of defiance; as though animated by a life of their own, the tails twitch and tremble. What aimed intensity of loathing! Another moment and surely there must be an explosion. But no; all of a sudden one of the two creatures turns away, hoists a hind leg in a more than fascist salute and, with the same fixed and focussed attention as it had given a moment before to its enemy, begins to make a lingual toilet. Animal love is as much at the mercy of distractions as animal hatred. The dumb creation lives a life made up of discrete and mutually irrelevant episodes. Such as it is, the consistency of human characters is due to the words upon which all human experiences are strung. We are purposeful because we can describe our feelings in remembrable words, can justify and rationalize our desires in terms of some kind of argument. Faced by an enemy we do not allow an itch to distract us from our emotions; the mere word "enemy" is enough to keep us reminded of our hatred, to convince us that we do well to be angry. Similarly the word "love" bridges for us those chasms of momentary indifference and boredom which gape from time to time between even the most ardent lovers. Feeling and desire provide us with our motive power; words give continuity to what we do and to a considerable extent determine our direction. Inappropriate and badly chosen words vitiate thought and lead to wrong or foolish conduct. Most ignorances are vincible, and in the greater number of cases stupidity is what the Buddha pronounced it to be, a sin. For, consciously or sub-consciously, it is with deliberation that we do not know or fail to understand—because incomprehension allows us, with a good conscience, to evade unpleasant obligations and responsibilities, because ignorance is the best excuse for going on doing what one likes, but ought not, to do. Our egotisms are incessantly fighting to preserve themselves, not only from external enemies, but also from the assaults of the other and better self with which they are so uncomfortably associated. Ignorance is egotism's most effective defence against that Dr. Jekyll in us who desires perfection; stupidity, its subtlest stratagem. If, as so often happens, we choose to give continuity to our experience by means of words which falsify the facts, this is because the falsification is somehow to our advantage as egotists.

Consider, for example, the case of war. War is enormously discreditable to those who order it to be waged and even to those who merely tolerate its existence. Furthermore, to developed sensibilities the facts of war are revolting and horrifying. To falsify these facts, and by so doing to make war seem less evil than it really is, and our own responsibility in tolerating war less heavy, is doubly to our advantage. By suppressing and distorting the truth, we protect our sensibilities and preserve our self-esteem. Now, language is, among other things, a device which men use for suppressing and distorting the truth. Finding the reality of war too unpleasant to contemplate, we create a verbal alternative to that reality, parallel with it, but in quality quite different from it. That which we contemplate thenceforward is not that to which we react emotionally and upon which we pass our moral judgments, is not war as it is in fact, but the fiction of war as it exists in our pleasantly falsifying verbiage. Our stupidity in using inappropriate language turns out, on analysis, to be the most refined cunning.

The most shocking fact about war is that its victims and its instruments are individual human beings, and that these individual human beings are condemned by the monstrous conventions of politics to murder or be murdered in quarrels not their own, to inflict upon the innocent and, innocent themselves of any crime against their enemies, to suffer cruelties of every kind.

The language of strategy and politics is designed, so

far as it is possible, to conceal this fact, to make it appear as though wars were not fought by individuals drilled to murder one another in cold blood and without provocation, but either by impersonal and therefore wholly non-moral and impassible forces, or else by personified abstractions.

Here are a few examples of the first kind of falsification. In place of "cavalrymen" or "foot-soldiers" military writers like to speak of "sabres" and "rifles." Here is a sentence from a description of the Battle of Marengo: "According to Victor's report, the French retreat was orderly; it is certain, at any rate, that the regiments held together, for the six thousand Austrian sabres found no opportunity to charge home." The battle is between sabres in line and muskets in échelon —a mere clash of ironmongery.

On other occasions there is no question of anything so vulgarly material as ironmongery. The battles are between Platonic ideas, between the abstractions of physics and mathematics. Forces interact; weights are flung into scales; masses are set in motion. Or else it is all a matter of geometry. Lines swing and sweep; are protracted or curved; pivot on a fixed point.

Alternatively the combatants are personal, in the sense that they are personifications. There is "the enemy," in the singular, making "his" plans, striking "his" blows. The attribution of personal characteristics to collectivities, to geographical expressions, to insti-

[87]

tutions, is a source, as we shall see, of endless confusions in political thought, of innumerable political mistakes and crimes. Personification in politics is an error which we make because it is to our advantage as egotists to be able to feel violently proud of our country and of ourselves as belonging to it, and to believe that all the misfortunes due to our own mistakes are really the work of the Foreigner. It is easier to feel violently towards a person than towards an abstraction; hence our habit of making political personifications. In some cases military personifications are merely special instances of political personifications. A particular collectivity, the army or the warring nation, is given the name and, along with the name, the attributes of a single person, in order that we may be able to love or hate it more intensely than we could do if we thought of it as what it really is: a number of diverse individuals. In other cases personification is used for the purpose of concealing the fundamental absurdity and monstrosity of war. What is absurd and monstrous about war is that men who have no personal quarrel should be trained to murder one another in cold blood. By personifying opposing armies or countries, we are able to think of war as a conflict between individuals. The same result is obtained by writing of war as though it were carried on exclusively by the generals in command and not by the private soldiers in their armies. ("Rennenkampf had pressed back von Schubert.") The implication in both cases is that war is indistinguishable from a bout of fisticuffs in a bar room. Whereas in reality it is profoundly different. A scrap between two individuals is forgivable; mass murder, deliberately organized, is a monstrous iniquity. We still choose to use war as an instrument of policy; and to comprehend the full wickedness and absurdity of war would therefore be inconvenient. For, once we understood, we should have to make some effort to get rid of the abominable thing. Accordingly, when we talk about war, we use a language which conceals or embellishes its reality. Ignoring the facts, so far as we possibly can, we imply that battles are not fought by soldiers, but by things, principles, allegories, personified collectivities, or (at the most human) by opposing commanders, pitched against one another in single combat. For the same reason, when we have to describe the processes and the results of war, we employ a rich variety of euphemisms. Even the most violently patriotic and militaristic are reluctant to call a spade by its own name. To conceal their intentions even from themselves, they make use of picturesque metaphors. We find them, for example, clamouring for war planes numerous and powerful enough to go and "destroy the hornets in their nests"— in other words, to go and throw thermite, high explosives and vesicants upon the inhabitants of neighbouring countries before they have time to come and do the same to us. And how reassuring is the language of historians and strategists! They write admiringly of those military geniuses who know "when to strike at the enemy's line" (a single combatant deranges the geometrical constructions of a personification); when to "turn his flank"; when to "execute an enveloping movement." As though they were engineers discussing the strength of materials and the distribution of stresses, they talk of abstract entities called "man power" and "fire power." They sum up the long-drawn sufferings and atrocities of trench warfare in the phrase, "a war of attrition"; the massacre and mangling of human beings is assimilated to the grinding of a lens.

A dangerously abstract word, which figures in all discussions about war, is "force." Those who believe in organizing collective security by means of military pacts against a possible aggressor are particularly fond of this word. "You cannot," they say, "have international justice unless you are prepared to impose it by force." "Peace-loving countries must unite to use force against aggressive dictatorships." "Democratic institutions must be protected, if need be, by force." And so on.

Now, the word "force," when used in reference to human relations, has no single, definite meaning. There is the "force" used by parents when, without resort to any kind of physical violence, they compel their children to act or refrain from acting in some particular way. There is the "force" used by attendants in an asylum when they try to prevent a maniac from hurting himself or others. There is the "force" used by the police when they control a crowd, and that other "force" which they use in a baton charge. And finally there is the "force" used in war. This, of course, varies with the technological devices at the disposal of the belligerents, with the policies they are pursuing, and with the particular circumstances of the war in question. But in general it may be said that, in war, "force" connotes violence and fraud used to the limit of the combatants' capacity.

Variations in quantity, if sufficiently great, produce variations in quality. The "force" that is war, particularly modern war, is very different from the "force" that is police action, and the use of the same abstract word to describe the two dissimilar processes is profoundly misleading. (Still more misleading, of course, is the explicit assimilation of a war, waged by allied League-of-Nations powers against an aggressor, to police action against a criminal. The first is the use of violence and fraud without limit against innocent and guilty alike; the second is the use of strictly limited violence and a minimum of fraud exclusively against the guilty.)

Reality is a succession of concrete and particular situations. When we think about such situations we should use the particular and concrete words which apply to them. If we use abstract words which apply equally well (and equally badly) to other, quite dis-

[91]

similar situations, it is certain that we shall think incorrectly.

Let us take the sentences quoted above and translate
the abstract word "force" into language that will render
(however inadequately) the concrete and particular
realities of contemporary warfare.

"You cannot have international justice, unless you
are prepared to impose it by force." Translated, this
becomes: "You cannot have international justice unless
you are prepared, with a view to imposing a just settlement, to drop thermite, high explosives and vesicants
upon the inhabitants of foreign cities and to have thermite, high explosives and vesicants dropped in return
upon the inhabitants of your cities." At the end of this
proceeding, justice is to be imposed by the victorious
party—that is, if there is a victorious party. It should be
remarked that justice was to have been imposed by the
victorious party at the end of the last war. But, unfortunately, after four years of fighting, the temper of the
victors was such that they were quite incapable of making a just settlement. The Allies are reaping in Nazi
Germany what they sowed at Versailles. The victors of
the next war will have undergone intensive bombard-
ments with thermite, high explosives and vesicants.
Will their temper be better than that of the Allies in
1918? Will they be in a fitter state to make a just settlement? The answer, quite obviously, is: No. It is psycho-

logically all but impossible that justice should be secured by the methods of contemporary warfare.

The next two sentences may be taken together. "Peace-loving countries must unite to use force against aggressive dictatorships. Democratic institutions must be protected, if need be, by force." Let us translate. "Peace-loving countries must unite to throw thermite, high explosives and vesicants on the inhabitants of countries ruled by aggressive dictators. They must do this, and of course abide the consequences, in order to preserve peace and democratic institutions." Two questions immediately propound themselves. First, is it likely that peace can be secured by a process calculated to reduce the orderly life of our complicated societies to chaos? And, second, is it likely that democratic institutions will flourish in a state of chaos? Again, the answers are pretty clearly in the negative.

By using the abstract word "force," instead of terms which at least attempt to describe the realities of war as it is to-day, the preachers of collective security through military collaboration disguise from themselves and from others, not only the contemporary facts, but also the probable consequences of their favourite policy. The attempt to secure justice, peace and democracy by "force" seems reasonable enough until we realize, first, that this non-committal word stands, in the circumstances of our age, for activities which can hardly fail to result in social chaos; and second, that the con sequences of social chaos are injustice, chronic warfare and tyranny. The moment we think in concrete and particular terms of the concrete and particular process called "modern war," we see that a policy which worked (or at least didn't result in complete disaster) in the past has no prospect whatever of working in the immediate future. The attempt to secure justice, peace and democracy by means of a "force," which means at this particular moment of history, thermite, high explosives and vesicants, is about as reasonable as the attempt to put out a fire with a colourless liquid that happens to be, not water, but petrol.

What applies to the "force" that is war applies in large measure to the "force" that is revolution. It seems inherently very unlikely that social justice and social peace can be secured by thermite, high explosives and vesicants. At first, it may be, the parties in a civil war would hesitate to use such instruments on their fellow-countrymen. But there can be little doubt that, if the conflict were prolonged (as it probably would be between the evenly balanced Right and Left of a highly industrialized society), the combatants would end by losing their scruples.

The alternatives confronting us seem to be plain enough. Either we invent and conscientiously employ a new technique for making revolutions and settling international disputes; or else we cling to the old technique and, using "force" (that is to say, thermite, high explosives and vesicants), destroy ourselves. Those who, for whatever motive, disguise the nature of the second alternative under inappropriate language, render the world a grave disservice. They lead us into one of the temptations we find it hardest to resist—the temptation to run away from reality, to pretend that facts are not what they are. Like Shelley (but without Shelley's acute awareness of what he was doing) we are perpetually weaving

> A shroud of talk to hide us from the sun
> Of this familiar life.

We protect our minds by an elaborate system of abstractions, ambiguities, metaphors and similes from the reality we do not wish to know too clearly; we lie to ourselves, in order that we may still have the excuse of ignorance, the alibi of stupidity and incomprehension, possessing which we can continue with a good conscience to commit and tolerate the most monstrous crimes:

> The poor wretch who has learned his only prayers
> From curses, who knows scarcely words enough
> To ask a blessing from his Heavenly Father,
> Becomes a fluent phraseman, absolute
> And technical in victories and defeats,
> And all our dainty terms for fratricide;
> Terms which we trundle smoothly o'er our tongues
> Like mere abstractions, empty sounds to which
> We join no meaning and attach no form!

As if the soldier died without a wound:
As if the fibres of this godlike frame
Were gored without a pang: as if the wretch
Who fell in battle, doing bloody deeds,
Passed off to Heaven translated and not killed;
As though he had no wife to pine for him,
No God to judge him.

The language we use about war is inappropriate, and its inappropriateness is designed to conceal a reality so odious that we do not wish to know it. The language we use about politics is also inappropriate; but here our mistake has a different purpose. Our principal aim in this case is to arouse and, having aroused, to rationalize and justify such intrinsically agreeable sentiments as pride and hatred, self-esteem and contempt for others. To achieve this end we speak about the facts of politics in words which more or less completely misrepresent them.

The concrete realities of politics are individual human beings, living together in national groups. Politicians—and to some extent we are all politicians—substitute abstractions for these concrete realities, and having done this, proceed to invest each abstraction with an appearance of concreteness by personifying it. For example, the concrete reality of which "Britain" is the abstraction consists of some forty-odd millions of diverse individuals living on an island off the west coast of Europe. The personification of this abstraction appears, in classical fancy-dress and holding a very large toasting fork, on the backside of our copper coinage; appears in verbal form, every time we talk about international politics. "Britain," the abstraction from forty millions of Britons, is endowed with thoughts, sensibilities and emotions, even with a sex—for, in spite of John Bull, the country is always a female.

Now, it is of course possible that "Britain" is more than a mere name—is an entity that possesses some kind of reality distinct from that of the individuals constituting the group to which the name is applied. But this entity, if it exists, is certainly not a young lady with a toasting fork; nor is it possible to believe (though some eminent philosophers have preached the doctrine) that it should possess anything in the nature of a personal will. One must agree with T. H. Green that "there can be nothing in a nation, however exalted its mission, or in a society, however perfectly organized, which is not in the persons composing the nation or the society. . . . We cannot suppose a national spirit and will to exist except as the spirit and will of individuals." But the moment we start resolutely thinking about our world in terms of individual persons we find ourselves at the same time thinking in terms of universality. "The great rational religions," writes Professor Whitehead, "are the outcome of the emergence of a religious consciousness that is universal, as distinguished from tribal, or even social. Because it is universal, it in-

troduces the note of solitariness." (And he might have
added that, because it is solitary, it introduces the note
of universality.) "The reason of this connection between universality and solitude is that universality is
a disconnection from immediate surroundings." And
conversely the disconnection from immediate surroundings, particularly such social surrounding as the tribe
or nation, the insistence on the person as the fundamental reality, leads to the conception of an all-embracing
unity.

A nation, then, may be more than a mere abstraction,
may possess some kind of real existence apart from its
constituent members. But there is no reason to suppose
that it is a person; indeed, there is every reason to suppose that it isn't. Those who speak as though it were
a person (and some go further than this and speak as
though it were a personal god), do so because it is to
their interest as egotists to make precisely this mistake.

In the case of the ruling class these interests are in
part material. The personification of the nation as a
sacred being, different from and superior to its constituent members, is merely (I quote the words of a
great French jurist, Léon Duguit) "a way of imposing
authority by making people believe it is an authority
de jure and not merely *de facto*." By habitually talking
of the nation as though it were a person with thoughts,
feelings and a will of its own, the rulers of a country
legitimate their own powers. Personification leads easily

to deification; and where the nation is deified, its government ceases to be a mere convenience, like drains or a telephone system, and, partaking in the sacredness of the entity it represents, claims to give orders by divine right and demands the unquestioning obedience due to a god. Rulers seldom find it hard to recognize their friends. Hegel, the man who elaborated an inappropriate figure of speech into a complete philosophy of politics, was a favourite of the Prussian government. *"Es ist,"* he had written, *"es ist der Gang Gottes in der Welt, das der Staat ist."* The decoration bestowed on him by Frederick William III was richly deserved.

Unlike their rulers, the ruled have no material interest in using inappropriate language about states and nations. For them, the reward of being mistaken is psychological. The personified and deified nation becomes, in the minds of the individuals composing it, a kind of enlargement of themselves. The superhuman qualities which belong to the young lady with the toasting fork, the young lady with plaits and a brass *soutiengorge,* the young lady in a Phrygian bonnet, are claimed by individual Englishmen, Germans and Frenchmen as being, at least in part, their own. *Dulce et decorum est pro patria mori.* But there would be no need to die, no need of war, if it had not been even sweeter to boast and swagger for one's country, to hate, despise, swindle and bully for it. Loyalty to the personified nation, or to the personified class or party, justifies the

loyal in indulging all those passions which good manners and the moral code do not allow them to display
in their relations with their neighbours. The personified entity is a being, not only great and noble, but also
insanely proud, vain and touchy; fiercely rapacious; a
braggart; bound by no considerations of right and
wrong. (Hegel condemned as hopelessly shallow all
those who dared to apply ethical standards to the activities of nations. To condone and applaud every iniquity
committed in the name of the State was to him a sign
of philosophical profundity.) Identifying themselves
with this god, individuals find relief from the con-
straints of ordinary social decency, feel themselves justified in giving rein, within duly prescribed limits, to
their criminal proclivities. As a loyal nationalist or
party-man, one can enjoy the luxury of behaving badly
with a good conscience.

The evil passions are further justified by another
linguistic error—the error of speaking about certain
categories of persons as though they were mere em-
bodied abstractions. Foreigners and those who disagree
with us are not thought of as men and women like ourselves and our fellow-countrymen; they are thought of
as representatives and, so to say, symbols of a class. In
so far as they have any personality at all, it is the personality we mistakenly attribute to their class—a personality that is, by definition, intrinsically evil. We

know that the harming or killing of men and women is wrong, and we are reluctant consciously to do what we know to be wrong. But when particular men and women are thought of merely as representatives of a class, which has previously been defined as evil and personified in the shape of a devil, then the reluctance to hurt or murder disappears. Brown, Jones and Robinson are no longer thought of as Brown, Jones and Robinson, but as heretics, gentiles, Yids, niggers, barbarians, Huns, communists, capitalists, fascists, liberals—whichever the case may be. When they have been called such names and assimilated to the accursed class to which the names apply, Brown, Jones and Robinson cease to be conceived as what they really are—human persons— and become for the users of this fatally inappropriate language mere vermin or, worse, demons whom it is right and proper to destroy as thoroughly and as painfully as possible. Wherever persons are present, questions of morality arise. Rulers of nations and leaders of parties find morality embarrassing. That is why they take such pains to depersonalize their opponents. All propaganda directed against an opposing group has but one aim: to substitute diabolical abstractions for concrete persons. The propagandist's purpose is to make one set of people forget that certain other sets of people are human. By robbing them of their personality, he puts them outside the pale of moral obligation. Mere

symbols can have no rights—particularly when that of
which they are symbolical is, by definition, evil.

Politics can become moral only on one condition:
that its problems shall be spoken of and thought about
exclusively in terms of concrete reality; that is to say,
of persons. To depersonify human beings and to per-
sonify abstractions are complementary errors which
lead, by an inexorable logic, to war between nations
and to idolatrous worship of the State, with consequent
governmental oppression. All current political thought
is a mixture, in varying proportions, between thought in
terms of concrete realities and thought in terms of depersonified symbols and personified abstractions. In the
democratic countries the problems of internal politics
are thought about mainly in terms of concrete reality;
those of external politics, mainly in terms of abstractions and symbols. In dictatorial countries the proportion of concrete to abstract and symbolic thought is
lower than in democratic countries. Dictators talk little
of persons, much of personified abstractions, such as the
Nation, the State, the Party, and much of depersonified
symbols, such as Yids, Bolshies, Capitalists. The stupidity of politicians who talk about a world of persons as
though it were not a world of persons is due in the
main to self-interest. In a fictitious world of symbols
and personified abstractions, rulers find that they can
rule more effectively, and the ruled, that they can
gratify instincts which the conventions of good man-

ners and the imperatives of morality demand that they should repress. To think correctly is the condition of behaving well. It is also in itself a moral act; those who would think correctly must resist considerable temptations.

Modern Fetishism

THE cult of relics was first rationalized in terms of
Christian theology by Cyril of Jerusalem. Unrational-
ized, it had, of course, existed since the time of the
earliest martyrs. Indeed, it had existed long before the
coming of Christianity. The Christian cult of relics is
merely a special case of an immemorial and universal
tendency to attribute *mana* to certain inanimate objects. The word fetish is derived from the Latin *facti-
tious,* and "was first used in connection with Africa by
the Portuguese discoverers of the last half of the fifteenth century; relics of saints, rosaries and images
were then abundant all over Europe and were regarded
as possessing magical virtue; they were termed by the
Portuguese *Feitiços* (i.e. charms). Early voyagers to
West Africa applied this term to the wooden figures,
stones, etc., regarded as the temporary residence of
gods or spirits, and to charms." There were good an-
thropologists four hundred years before the invention
of anthropology.

Relic worship was officially abolished by all the
Protestant reformers. But just as it preceded, so too
this cult has survived, Catholicism. Where such deep-
rooted tendencies as fetishism are concerned, all that
reformers can hope to abolish is the temporary form,

not the abiding substance. Officially rejected by theologians, fetishism does not cease to exist. All that happens is that, from being public and respectable, its manifestations become secret, personal and slightly shameful. Defined in terms of sociology, magic is merely unauthorized, private religion. During the war there were probably more fetishes in use among Protestants and agnostics than in the whole of Africa and Melanesia, more even than in the Europe of the later Middle Ages, when churches numbered their relics by the thousand. Nor, of course, has the cult of public fetishes and avowable relics altogether disappeared; it has merely moved away from the churches and established itself elsewhere. Thus, the flag has taken the place, as a cult object, of the cross; and in the icon corner one sees the image, not of a saint, but of the local dictator or a favourite political author. Even the ancient cult of bones and mummies has been laicized and brought up to date. The graves of the martyrs of the Commune are yearly visited by great crowds of Parisian workmen; and, in the Kremlin, stuffed and refrigerated, Lenin is preserved as an object of adoration for millions of pious atheists. Nor are benighted foreigners the only modern relic worshippers; for at this present moment (1933) we in England are being simultaneously invited, as Maecenases, and, as tax-payers, compelled to contribute towards the purchase, as a national fetish, of the Codex Sinaiticus.

"There are people," the Director of the British Museum is reported as saying, "people who criticize the spending of such a large sum of money at a time like this; but the offer by the Government (of £1 for every £1 subscribed by the public) shows that they realize the importance of watching over the intellectual needs as well as the material needs of the nation." And Sir Frederic Kenyon concludes a letter to *The Times* with the sentence: "Where millions are spent on the material needs and amusements of the people, may not £100,000 be properly spent upon their minds and souls?" To this question I hasten to return an enthusiastic affirmative. I should like to see a great deal more than a hundred thousand pounds spent on people's "minds and souls." But the money spent on the Codex Sinaiticus is not money spent on "minds and souls"; it is money spent on a relic, a mere *feitiço*. And the Government which helps to purchase such *feitiços* is not "watching over the intellectual interests of the nation"; it is indulging, at the tax-payer's expense, in a costly gesture of superstition and idolatry.

All spiritual values may be catalogued under one or other of the three heads: Good, True, Beautiful. Let us dispassionately consider the Codex Sinaiticus and try to estimate its position under each of these three categories.

I will begin with Beauty. Where does the Codex stand in the hierarchy of things beautiful? Obviously, very low. True, the large uncial script in which it is written is pleasant enough; but the book is not and does not claim to be a work of art. At the best, it is a pretty little piece of competent craftsmanship.

Let us consider it now in relation to Truth. Its truth value *was* very considerable; for the study of the manuscript led to the discovery of a number of interesting and hitherto unknown facts about the text of the Bible. But is there any reason to suppose that further study will elicit any new facts of importance? And, for the purposes of scholarship, does the original manuscript possess any marked and significant superiority over photographic reproductions? And, finally, what is there to prevent the searchers after more historical truth from going to Russia to look for it?

We come now to the category of Goodness. Of what makes for goodness the Codex clearly possesses no more than any other copy of the Bible. Indeed, for practical purposes, it actually possesses less than the Authorized Version you can buy for five shillings at the nearest bookseller's. For the five-shilling Bible is comprehensible and available; whereas the Codex is kept locked up in a box and can be read only by experts. Its light is permanently under a bushel. The ordinary visitor to the British Museum looks at it through two intervening layers, one of plate glass, the other of his own ignorance. What he understands of the Codex is *nil*. What he feels, if he feels anything when he examines it, is a vague sentimental awe, mingled with self-satisfaction. The Codex for him is just an equivalent—yet another equivalent—of Shakespeare's birthplace. Having peered at it and perhaps taken off his hat to it, he goes away with the comfortable conviction that he has done his duty by Culture and Religion. A bus trip to Stratford-on-Avon is for thousands of Shakespeare's fellow-countrymen sufficient excuse for never looking into *Macbeth* or *Hamlet*. They feel that they have done enough by paying an idolatrous visit to the shrine of the Bard; to read him would be a work of supererogation. It is now to be the same with the Bible. The Codex Sinaiticus stands to the Bible in exactly the same relation as Anne Hathaway's cottage to the works of Shakespeare. If you regard idolatry as a good thing, then you will wholeheartedly approve of the purchase of the Codex. I happen to regard idolatry as a very bad thing—all the worse for the fact that it has roots that go deep into our human and sub-human nature.

The general conclusions which impose themselves are these. The Codex is not beautiful. Its truth value seems to be pretty well exhausted; and anyhow such truth value as it still does possess is as readily available in facsimile as in the original, and in Leningrad as in London. Finally, its powers to propagate the good which, in common with all other copies of the Bible, it contains, is exceptionally, almost uniquely, small. On the contrary, its power to propagate a habit of stupid and irrational idolatry is exceptionally great.

In view of all this, one may be permitted to wonder how precisely "the intellectual needs of the nation" are being served by the acquisition of this costly fetish; or in what sense, other than a purely Pickwickian one, it can be said that our hundred thousand pounds are being spent upon the people's "minds and souls." The truth of the matter is that the purchase is wholly unjustifiable in terms of a rationally idealistic philosophy. Spiritually, the Codex is valueless. If it is precious, it is precious only for its rarity, its associations and because it is superstitiously felt to contain some kind of *mana*.

There is in almost all human beings a stamp-collector and a fetish-worshipper; and it is to these personages that the Codex makes its appeal. Our hundred thousand pounds have bought us an object which is a mixture between the British Guiana Two-Cent, 1851, and the Thaumaturgical Arm of St. Francis Xavier.

The tendencies to superstition and mere collecting are, as I have said, almost universal; they are not for that reason rational or good. A Government which professes to care about "the mind and soul of the people," to watch over "the intellectual needs of the nation," has no business to spend public money for the gratification of these absurd and always slightly discreditable passions. Its business is to encourage all manifestations of the Good, the True and the Beautiful.

[109]

The Government's action seems the more unjustifiable when we reflect that it has consistently put forward the plea of economy as an excuse for cutting down the grants (small enough, heaven knows, at the best of times) for scientific research. "It has been decided to concentrate available funds on the work of the most immediate practical value to industry, leaving to happier times the expansion of work, of which the results could only be available at some more distant date." In other and less hideously official words, it has been decided that the pursuit of truth for truth's sake is too expensive. But when it comes to buying a stamp-collector's fetish, fifty thousand pounds of other people's money are stumped up without the smallest hesitation.

What applies to Truth applies also to Beauty. The Government is too poor to spend more than a miserably small sum on the acquisition of beautiful objects, or on the encouragement of men and women capable of adding to the existing store of artistic beauty. But it has money to spare for idolatry and mere bibliophily. Our National Church had the good sense to abolish the cult of relics; our National Government has now officially reversed the policy of these reforming idealists, and the tax-payer is to find fifty thousand pounds for the purchase of a fetish.

Literature and Examinations

IT HAPPENS on the average once every three or four months. The postman drops into my letter-box an envelope addressed in an unfamiliar writing and postmarked anywhere from Oslo to Algiers. Opening it, I find a letter, sometimes in strange English, sometimes in one of the foreign languages with which an ordinarily cultured person is supposed to be familiar. The writer begins by an apology. He (or as often she) is sorry to trouble me, but the fact is that he or she is a student at the university of X or Y or Z, and that, in order to obtain his or her Doctorate of Letters, Diploma of Pedagogy, Bachelorship of Modern Languages, Aggregation to the University, or whatever the thing may happen to be called, he or she is writing a thesis about my books—or more often about some particular aspect of my books, such as their style, their construction, the influence upon them of other books, the idea of God in them, their *Weltanschauung* or *Geschlechtsphilosophie*. This being so, will I kindly furnish biographical material, a bibliography of all the reviews and criticisms written in every language, together with copies of such books as the writer happens to have been unable to obtain. In many cases the letter ends with an appeal to my better feelings: will I please do everything that is

[111]

asked of me, because, if I don't, the writer will be unable to obtain the coveted post at the local University, Lycée, Gymnasium, Preparatoria, or what not, and will have to be content with a job as a teacher in an elementary school.

My feelings when one of these letters arrives are extremely mixed. That I should be treated as though I were a classical author of some earlier century, simultaneously amuses and depresses me, tickles my self-esteem and at the same time punctures it. I like very naturally to think that I am being read; but the idea that I am being *studied* fills me, after the first outburst of laughter, with a deepening gloom. There is something extremely disagreeable about being treated as though one were dead when one supposes—perhaps (and this is the really disquieting thought) mistakenly —that one is still very much alive. Nor is the anticipation of posthumous Fame any compensating satisfaction. For to be sufficiently famous to deserve elaborate study in a modern university is quite humiliatingly easy. Merely to have published is now a sufficient claim to academic attention. As time passes and the numbers of aspirants to diplomas and doctorates continues to pile up, it becomes increasingly difficult to find any significant aspect of a good writer's work which has not already formed the subject of a thesis. The candidate for academic honours has no choice but to study the insignificant aspects of a good writer's work or else the work, not yet explored, because universally deemed not worth exploring, of a bad writer. Universities do me the honour of treating me as though I were defunct and a classic; but it is an honour, alas, that I share with Flecknoe and Pixéricourt, with Hofmann von Hofmannswaldau and Nahum Tate.

Walter Raleigh used to say that the teaching of literature always verged on the absurd. He understated the case. The teaching of literature often oversteps the verge and tumbles headlong into the most grotesque absurdity. It is absurd, for example, that students should be forced to spend months and years of their lives on the study of writers who are, by universal consent, of no importance whatsoever. It is equally absurd that they should spend months and years on the study of unimportant aspects of the work of good writers. Very many of the scores of theses produced each year in the various universities of the world are totally pointless. But the teaching of literature produces other absurdities no less monstrous than the learned thesis about a trivial theme. Comparatively few students aspire to specialized learning. For every doctor there are hundreds of bachelors. These obtain their degrees by retailing at second hand a little of the learning and a good deal of the literary criticism of others. Fashions in criticism change, and the candidate must be able to regurgitate the judgment in vogue in academic circles at the time of his ordeal. Success in literary examinations comes to those who know, among other things, what formulae happen, momentarily, to be correct.

What applies to literature applies also to the fine arts. For there are now academic institutions which actually give people degrees in art—minor degrees for those who know a list of dates and can repeat the proper ritual *mantras* about pictures and churches and statues; higher degrees to those who undertake profound original researches into the work of the deservedly neglected artists of the past.

The ultimate cause for this on the whole deplorable state of things is economic. Degrees have a definite cash value. The possession of a given diploma may make all the difference (as my correspondents so often point out in their appeals to my better feelings) between low wages and a low social position in an elementary school and good wages, with considerable social prestige, in the hierarchy of secondary education. Literature and fine arts figure in most curricula at the present time; men and women aspire to teach these subjects; headmasters and education authorities want to be able to distinguish between those who are "qualified" to teach them and those who are not; universities oblige by creating faculties of literature and fine arts, complete with all the apparatus of diplomas, degrees and doctorates.

Now it is obviously necessary that, for examination purposes, literature and the fine arts should convert themselves, at any rate partially, into parodies of the exact sciences. Literature and art appeal as much to the affective and conative as to the merely cognitive side of man's being. But if you are going to give people marks for literature and art, you must ask them questions that can be answered correctly or incorrectly, you must set them tasks which can be performed only by dint of persevering industriousness. Candidates for the lower degrees will be required, like candidates for the lower degrees in chemistry, say, or biology, to read text-books and do "practical" work. (In the case of literature, this practical work consists, like the theoretical work, in reading. But whereas theoretical reading is a reading of text-books, practical reading is a reading of the original texts.) Candidates for the higher degrees are expected, like the prospective doctor of science, to do a piece of original research and record their discoveries in a thesis. Even the laboratory methods of exact science are parodied. Literature does not lend itself to being weighed or measured; but at least its material embodiments can be minutely observed and accurately reproduced. The editing of texts has become a branch of microscopy.

It is quite true, of course, that literature and the fine arts have non-literary and non-artistic aspects. They provide important documents in the fields, for example, of social and economic history, of psychology, of philology and the philosophy of language. Moreover, writers and artists employ techniques of expression which profitably lend themselves to scientific analysis. Thus, the *alchimie du verbe,* as Rimbaud called it, can be made to yield some at least of its strange secrets; the geometry and optics of picture-making are worthy of the most serious study. In so far as they are not literature and not art, literature and art can be subjected most fruitfully to the methods of science. And, in effect, much excellent work in history, psychology and so forth has been done by the writers of supposedly literary and artistic theses. All would be well if universities would insist that such work is frankly historical, psychological and the rest, and that it has little or nothing to do with literature as literature, or with art as art. But unfortunately this necessary distinction is not drawn. Under the present dispensation, absurd pseudo-scientific research—into the date, shall we say, of John Chalkhill's second marriage, into the indebtedness of Shadwell to Molière—is as freely encouraged as genuinely scientific research carried out for the purpose of establishing significant relations between one set of facts and another. Moreover, the scientifically treatable, non-literary and non-artistic aspects of literature and art are kept hopelessly mixed up with their purely literary and artistic aspects. Candidates are given marks for displaying symptoms, not merely of knowledge, but also of sensibility and judgment—other people's sensibility, in general practice, and other people's judgment. Perfectly good scientific work has to be accompanied by the repetition of the *mantras* of fashionable criticism. The aesthetic heart must be worn, all through the weary hours of the final examination, palpitating on the sleeve. Every candidate for the bachelorship or doctorate is expected to overflow with the pious phrases of "appreciation." The present examination system is calculated to produce the literary and artistic equivalents of Tartufe and Pecksniff.

That men should hypocritically pay the tribute that philistinism owes to culture is greatly to be desired. The tendency to be realistic and hard-boiled is as dangerous in the sphere of culture as in that of politics. You cannot appeal to the humanitarianism of a fascist who starts out with the realistic assumption that because, in fact, might generally prevails, might is therefore right and should never make any concessions at all. Similarly you cannot appeal to the cultural piety of a low-brow who thinks that, because most human beings are like himself, low-browism is therefore right and ought to triumph over high-browism. Without moral hypocrisy and intellectual snobbery, the decencies of life would lead a most precarious existence.

Intellectual snobbery, I insist, is an excellent thing; but, as of all excellent things, there may be too much of it. An examination system that encourages the candidate for a degree to adorn his non-literary and non-artistic knowledge of literature and art with a veneer

[117]

of "appreciative" cant is calculated to produce an excessive number of cultural Pecksniffs, each convinced, on the strength of his diploma, that he is always right. Under a more rational system of education, degrees in literature and art would not be given. Literary and artistic documents would, however, be used as the material of scientific researches in other fields. Feats of mere industry for industry's sake, such as the compilation of theses about writers valueless from a literary point of view and of no particular historical, psychological, economic or other interest, would be discouraged. The application of exact scientific methods to the typography of old books could safely be left to the voluntary enthusiasm of Nature's philatelists and crossword puzzlers. Meanwhile, of course, efforts would be made to encourage students to read and to look at works of art. Groups would be organized for the reading of papers and the discussion of literary and artistic problems. There would also be exercises in the art of writing clearly and correctly. In this way the natural sensibilities of the students might be developed, and the tendency, so much encouraged by the examination system, to mug up other people's judgments and repeat them, mechanically and without reflection, severely discouraged. At the same time students would be able to feel that their scientific work—the study of the significant non-literary and non-artistic aspects of literary and artistic documents—was genuinely valuable and en-

[118]

lightening, not the mere parody of scientific work that, too often, they are expected to do at present.

As things stand at present, it would be very difficult to make the kind of changes I have indicated above, for the simple reason that there are very many people who, for economic reasons, *want* degrees in literature and the fine arts. The employers of academic labour regard such degrees as qualifications for comparatively well-paid posts. It will be impossible to change the existing examination system until they have been educated to think differently.

English Snobbery

AFTER a holiday from periodical literature, I am always staggered, when I get back to a well-stocked reading-room, by the inordinate snobbery of the English press. In no other country do so many newspapers devote so large a proportion of their space to a chronicle of the activities of the merely rich or the merely ennobled. Nowhere else in Europe is gossip-writing a highly paid and creditable profession; nowhere else would such a headline as "Peer's Cousin in Car Smash" be even imaginable. And where else but in England can one find three expensive but flourishing weeklies devoted to absolutely nothing but the life of the rich and the titled? Not to mention the several other weeklies in which this absorbing theme occupies, not indeed an exclusive, but still an important place.

On whom, one wonders, do these expensive weeklies live? To some extent, of course, upon the elect whom they exhibit walking in the Park with friends, attending race-meetings, eating dinners for Incurables or dancing in fancy dress for Crippled Children. Upon those, in a word, whose photographs have actually been published in their pages and upon all such as may reasonably hope, one memorable day, to achieve the same distinction. The ranks of the snapshot-worthy have recently been swelled by a considerable mass of new recruits. In the past, only the really rich, the definitely titled, the unequivocally West End stars were ever photographed. To-day, in search, no doubt, of new subscribers, the exploiters of snobbery go forth and fairly rake the County hedges and ditches for their material. Captain and Mrs. Knapweed-Knapweed with their daughter Angelica ("Peggy") are now portrayed, walking with friends at hunt steeplechases. A sad decline. But business is business. There are not enough earls or actresses. The Knapweed-Knapweeds must be called in to fill the void.

There are in England only one hundred thousand persons whose income exceeds two thousand pounds a year. Of these not more, I imagine, than ten thousand can even hope to qualify for a place in the snobbery-exploiting weeklies. Compared with the earls and the actresses, the Knapweed-Knapweeds are numerous; but they are not a circulation—and a circulation is precisely what the snobbery-exploiting weeklies possess. These weeklies must be read—disinterestedly, in a certain sense—by thousands for whom the possibility of personally figuring among the walkers-in-parks, or even among their anonymous friends, is simply unimaginable. There is a snobbery which, like virtue, is its own reward.

What precisely, one speculates, is the nature of that reward? For most of the readers of the gossip columns their wealthier contemporaries take rank with film stars and the heroes and heroines of novels. Reading of their activities, they enjoy vicariously the pleasures—those amazingly boring and unvariegated pleasures—of the rich. What is quotidian reality for earls, actresses and Knapweed-Knapweeds is for them a delightful, compensatory fiction.

There are others, no doubt, who read for the sake of sarcastically laughing. How many? It is impossible to say. They cannot constitute a majority of newspaper readers; for if they did there would very soon be no more society or gossip columns to laugh at. One is forced rather reluctantly to the conclusion that most readers either positively enjoy the snobbery columns of their newspapers, or else accept them with resignation, as part of the established order of things, like the income tax or rain in summer.

Why should the English public proclaim itself so much more keenly interested in the doings of the rich and the titled than the public in other countries? Attachment to tradition may be invoked as one of the causes. The habit, established in long-past days when a title really meant something, of regarding a lord with a kind of awed curiosity still persists in a vestigial state, like the spiritual equivalent of the vermiform appendix. Elsewhere revolution has roughly excised this survival from the days of feudalism. But the last English revolution, that of 1688, was itself made by the aristoc-

racy; instead of being cut out, the appendix rooted itself more firmly in the national consciousness. Another
point: the English standard of living is high. There is
an immense sub-middle class with enough money to
preserve it from rancorous envy of the rich, but not
enough to preserve it from boredom; it needs vicarious
compensations and manages to find them in the gossip
columns.

So much for the snobbery of the people who can
never hope to be caught by the camera walking in the
Park or drinking champagne for charity. We have now
to consider the snobbery of those who have actually
enjoyed this privilege. It is, of course, among these last
that the passion is most intense. The objects of snobbery are themselves the greatest snobs.

That which, for the vulgar, is no more than a survival
of something which once was useful, takes rank in the
interior economy of the elect as a vital organ—no mere
appendix, but an essential part of the aristocratic intes-
tine. For the rich and the titled, snobbery is not a superfluous luxury, but a necessity; their self-regarding instincts impose it upon them. They are snobs because,
like the rest of us, they are egotists. They admire the
rich and titled for the good reason that the rich and
titled are themselves.

This kind of snobbery exists wherever there is a
privileged class. In other countries, however, gestures
of aristocratic and plutocratic self-admiration are not

received with sympathy, therefore are not made, except in private. For reasons which I have tried to explain above, large numbers of the English derive from gossip column and society weekly a deep satisfaction. They are prepared to listen to the privileged class congratulating itself. Where ears are willing, talk tends to be loud and long. The snobbery of the ruling classes in England is allowed the freest possible expression. Daily it takes the offered opportunity.

Time and the Machine

TIME, as we know it, is a very recent invention. The modern time-sense is hardly older than the United States. It is a by-product of industrialism—a sort of psychological analogue of synthetic perfumes and aniline dyes.

Time is our tyrant. We are chronically aware of the moving minute hand, even of the moving second hand. We have to be. There are trains to be caught, clocks to be punched, tasks to be done in specified periods, records to be broken by fractions of a second, machines that set the pace and have to be kept up with. Our consciousness of the smallest units of time is now acute. To us, for example, the moment 8.17 A.M. means something—something very important, if it happens to be the starting time of our daily train. To our ancestors, such an odd eccentric instant was without significance—did not even exist. In inventing the locomotive, Watt and Stevenson were part inventors of time.

Another time-emphasizing entity is the factory and its dependent, the office. Factories exist for the purpose of getting certain quantities of goods made in a certain time. The old artisan worked as it suited him with the result that consumers generally had to wait for the goods they had ordered from him. The factory is a

[125]

device for making workmen hurry. The machine revolves so often each minute; so many movements have to be made, so many pieces produced each hour. Result: the factory worker (and the same is true, *mutatis mutandis*, of the office worker) is compelled to know time in its smallest fractions. In the hand-work age there was no such compulsion to be aware of minutes and seconds.

Our awareness of time has reached such a pitch of intensity that we suffer acutely whenever our travels take us into some corner of the world where people are not interested in minutes and seconds. The unpunctuality of the Orient, for example, is appalling to those who come freshly from a land of fixed meal-times and regular train services. For a modern American or Englishman, waiting is a psychological torture. An Indian accepts the blank hours with resignation, even with satisfaction. He has not lost the fine art of doing nothing. Our notion of time as a collection of minutes, each of which must be filled with some business or amusement, is wholly alien to the Oriental, just as it was wholly alien to the Greek. For the man who lives in a pre-industrial world, time moves at a slow and easy pace; he does not care about each minute, for the good reason that he has not been made conscious of the existence of minutes.

This brings us to a seeming paradox. Acutely aware of the smallest constituent particles of time—of time, as measured by clock-work and train arrivals and the revolutions of machines—industrialized man has to a great extent lost the old awareness of time in its larger divisions. The time of which we have knowledge is artificial, machine-made time. Of natural, cosmic time, as it is measured out by sun and moon, we are for the most part almost wholly unconscious. Pre-industrial people know time in its daily, monthly and seasonal rhythms. They are aware of sunrise, noon and sunset of the full moon and the new; of equinox and solstice; of spring and summer, autumn and winter. All the old religions, including Catholic Christianity, have insisted on this daily and seasonal rhythm. Pre-industrial man was never allowed to forget the majestic movement of cosmic time.

Industrialism and urbanism have changed all this. One can live and work in a town without being aware of the daily march of the sun across the sky; without ever seeing the moon and stars. Broadway and Piccadilly are our Milky Way; our constellations are outlined in neon tubes. Even changes of season affect the townsman very little. He is the inhabitant of an artificial universe that is, to a great extent, walled off from the world of nature. Outside the walls, time is cosmic and moves with the motion of sun and stars. Within, it is an affair of revolving wheels and is measured in seconds and minutes—at its longest, in eight-hour days and six-day weeks. We have a new consciousness; but it has been purchased at the expense of the old consciousness.

New-fashioned Christmas

THE name is still the same; but the thing is almost unrecognizably different from what Charles Dickens meant by "Christmas." For example, there was no tree at Dingley Dell, and, except for five shillings to Sam Weller, not a single present was given. Christmas, for Mr. Pickwick and his friends, was an affair of copious eating and still more copious drinking, interrupted by bouts of home-made fun and purely domestic horse-play.

For us, three generations later, the word connotes the Prince Consort's imported Teutonic evergreen; connotes all those endless presents, which it is such a burden to buy and such an embarrassment to receive; connotes restaurants, dance halls, theatres, cabarets—all the highly organized, professional entertainments provided by the astute business men who run the amusement industry. Only the name connects the new-fashioned Christmas with the Pickwickian festival.

The tree, of course, was a mere accident. If Queen Victoria had married a Frenchman we should probably be giving one another *étrennes* and ushering in the year with a series of calls on the most remote and the most personally antipathetic of our innumerable relations. (Relations, in France, *are* innumerable.) As it was, she took to herself a prince from the land of tannen-baums. It is therefore to a tannenbaum's green branches, and upon Christmas Day, that we attach our gifts.

The tree, I repeat, was an accident, a thing outside the realm of determinism, a product of personal idio-syncrasy. But all the other changes in our Christmas habits, which have taken place since Dickens wrote of Dingley Dell, are the results of great impersonal proc-esses. During Dickens's lifetime, and still more rapidly after his death, industrial production enormously and continuously increased. But production cannot increase unless there is a corresponding increase in consump-tion. It became necessary to stimulate consumption, to provide the home public with reasons, or, better still, with compelling unreasons, for consuming. Hence the rise of advertisement, and hence the gradual and, as time went on, the more and more deliberate canaliza-tion into industrially profitable channels of all such common human impulses and emotions as lent them-selves to the process.

The producer who succeeds in thus canalizing some universal human urge opens up for himself and his successors an inexhaustible gold mine. Thus, art and industry have flourished from time immemorial in the rich soil of bereavement and the fear of death. Wed-dings have been almost as profitable to commerce as funerals, and within the last few years an American man of genius has discovered how even filial affection may be made a justification for increased consumption; the florists and candy manufacturers of the United States have reason to bless the inventor of Mother's Day.

The love of excitement is as deeply planted in human nature as the love of a mother; the desire for change, for novelty, for a relief from the monotony of every day, as strong as sexual desire or the terror of death. Men have instituted festivals and holidays to satisfy these cravings. Mr. Pickwick's Christmas was a typical feast day of the old style—a time of jollification and excitement, a gaudily glittering "captain jewel in the carcanet" of grey, uneventful days. Psychologically, it performed its function. Not economically, however— that is, so far as *we* are concerned. The Pickwickian Christmas did very little to stimulate consumption; it was mainly a gratuitous festivity. A few vintners and distillers and poulterers were the only people whom it greatly profited financially. This was a state of things which an ever-increasingly efficient industrialism could not possibly afford to tolerate. Christmas, accordingly, was canalized. The deep festal impulse of man was harnessed and made to turn a very respectable little wheel in the mills of industry. To-day Christmas is an important economic event. The distributors of goods spend large sums in advertising potential gifts, and (since the man who pays the piper calls the tune) the newspapers reinforce their advertisements by fostering a notion that the mutual goodwill of modern Christians can be expressed only by the exchange of manufactured articles.

The last thirty years have witnessed the promotion of innkeeping and showmanship to the rank of major commercial enterprises. Major commercial enterprises spend money on advertising. Therefore, newspapers are always suggesting that a good time can be enjoyed only by those who take what is offered them by entertainment manufacturers. The Dickensian Christmas-at-Home receives only perfunctory lip-service from a press which draws a steady income from the catering and amusement trades. Home-made fun is gratuitous, and gratuitousness is something which an industrialized world cannot afford to tolerate.

Historical Generalizations

Mr. Dawson calls his study[1] of the Dark Ages "an Introduction to the History of European Unity." The words ring a trifle ironically in the ear. That mediaeval unity of culture and religion to which Mr. Dawson's period led up never prevented good Catholic Europeans from cutting one another's throats. Christendom may have been one; but it was in a chronic condition of civil war. What is the value, we may ask, of such a purely platonic unity? What, indeed, is the meaning of the term? To some extent, at least, historians must be behaviourists. If at any given epoch men behave as though they were not united, then surely the society which they constitute can hardly be called a unity. Can the spiritual substance of unity possess reciprocal throat-cutting as one of its accidents and still remain itself? It is a nice question.

We may be at one with Mr. Dawson in "feeling once more the need for spiritual or at least moral unity," we may be dissatisfied with "a civilization that finds its unity in external and superficial things and ignores the deeper needs of man's spiritual nature"; but we must also bear in mind that political and economic unifica-

[1] *The Making of Europe,* by Christopher Dawson. London, Sheed and Ward, 1932. 12s. 6d.

[132]

tion, though "external and superficial," are of equal importance with cultural and spiritual unification. Indeed, the latter cannot be said to exist (except in a platonic and Pickwickian sense) without the former. The unity of mediaeval Christendom never manifested itself as an observable fact of experience; throat-cutting and political disunion made the manifestation impossible.

Mr. Dawson's title-page has delayed me too long. It is time to consider his book. This is quite admirable. Following Mr. Dawson's light, the unspecialized reader finds himself able to thread his way through those obscure corridors of time which extend from the fall of the Roman Empire to the Norman Conquest. The Dark Ages lose their darkness, take on form and significance. Thanks to Mr. Dawson's erudition and his gift of marshalling facts, we begin to have a notion of what it is all about.

The book is short, the period long. Mr. Dawson has had to select, compress and generalize in order to carry us through the centuries at the required speed. For the most part, he generalizes with a sobriety and a caution worthy of the highest praise. We meet, in his pages, with none of those "deep" metaphysical hypotheses, in terms of which some modern German historians have so excitingly and so unjustifiably interpreted the course of past events. Mr. Dawson is an intellectual ascetic who conscientiously refrains from indulging in such delicious but dangerous extravagances. For this he deserves all our gratitude.

Occasionally, it is true, Mr. Dawson makes a generalization with which I find myself (with all the diffidence of an unlearned dilettante) disagreeing. For example, "the modern European," he says, "is accustomed to look on society as essentially concerned with the present life, and with material needs, and on religion as an influence on the moral life of the individual. But to the Byzantine, and indeed to mediaeval man in general, the primary society was the religious one, and economic and secular affairs were a secondary consideration." In confirmation of this Mr. Dawson quotes, among other documents, a passage from the writings of St. Gregory Nazianzen on the interest universally displayed by his fourth-century contemporaries in theology. "The money changer will talk about the Begotten and the Unbegotten, instead of giving you your money, and if you want a bath, the bath keeper assures you that the Son surely proceeds from nothing." What Mr. Dawson does not mention is that, in another passage, this same Gregory reproaches the people of Constantinople with an excessive interest in chariot racing—an interest which, in the time of Justinian, a century and a half later, had become so maniacally passionate that Greens and Blues were murdering one another by hundreds and even thousands. Again we must apply the Behaviourist test. If men behave as though they took a passionate interest in something—and it is difficult to prove your devotion to a cause more effectively than by killing and being killed for it—then we must presume that that interest is genuine, a primary rather than a secondary consideration. The actual facts seem to demonstrate that some Byzantines were passionately interested in religion, others (or perhaps they were the same) were no less passionately interested in sport. At any rate, they behaved about both in the same way and were as ready to undergo martyrdom for their favourite jockey as for their favourite article in the Athanasian Creed. The trouble with such generalizations as that of Mr. Dawson is that they ignore the fact that society is never homogeneous and that human beings belong to many different mental species. This seems to be true even in primitive societies displaying the maximum of "co-consciousness" on the part of their members. Thus, the anthropologist, Radin, well known for his work among the Red Indians, has come to the conclusion that monotheistic beliefs are correlated with a specific temperament and so may be expected to crop up with a certain specific frequency, irrespective of culture. If this is true (and it is in accord with our personal experience of civilized life and with the results of anthropological research among primitive peoples), then what becomes of a generalization like Mr. Dawson's? Obviously, it falls to the ground. You can no more indict an age than you can a nation.

[135]

At every epoch some people are primarily interested in the things of the other world, some in the things of this world. The chief difference between a religious and a non-religious epoch would seem to be this: that in a religious epoch those whose main interest is in secular affairs tend to justify that interest in terms of theology (the Greens would hate the Blues for being unorthodox, and vice versa) and to find transcendental motives for sublunary action. In a non-religious age, this-worldly people are free to believe that the things in which they take an interest are intrinsically valuable, while naturally religious people are driven to look for this-worldly justifications (social and political) for their other-worldliness. Sociologically considered, the superiority of a religious to a non-religious epoch lies in the fact that people have more and more powerful motives for action. The trouble is that you can never be certain whether the action undertaken for religious reasons is going to be good or bad. A characteristic example of mixed action undertaken for religious motives is provided by the pious Mgr. de Belzunce who distinguished himself during the great plague of Marseilles as much by his acts of heroic Christian charity as by his revolting sectarian intolerance.

It took the Lynds and their assistants eighteen months of intensive personal investigation to bring together the materials for their classic study of a modern industrial community, "Middletown." This community, as it happened, was a particularly homogeneous one; the Lynds' researches showed that anyone born in Middletown with unusual abilities took the earliest possible opportunity of going somewhere else. Nevertheless, even in this more than ordinarily homogeneous town, the investigators met with many distinct human types, many fundamentally different attitudes towards the problems of life. There existed, of course, a behaviour pattern which was, statistically, normal. But the departures from the norm were considerable. After reading "Middletown" one becomes more than ever suspicious of the generalizations of historians about the character and mentality of the men and women of past ages. For upon what are these generalizations based? Upon an originally inadequate documentation further reduced by the ravages of time to a random collection of literary and archaeological odds and ends. As statements about the past, such generalizations are therefore of dubious value. They must always be taken with a grain of salt; at best they are only half or three-quarter truths. If they have value, it is as stimulants to make us think about the present. Generalized history is a branch of speculation, connected (often rather arbitrarily and uneasily) with certain facts about the past. Circumstances alter, each age must think its own thoughts. Not until there is a settled and definitive world order can there be such a thing as a settled and definitive version of human history.

[137]

Crébillon the Younger

PROPHECY is mainly interesting for the light it throws
on the age in which it is uttered. The Apocalypse, for
example, tells us how a Christian felt about the world
at the end of the first century. Manifestly ludicrous as
a forecast, Mercier's *L'An 2240* is worth reading, because it shows us what were the ideals of an earnest and
rather stupid Frenchman in the year 1770. And the
ideals of an earnest and very intelligent Englishman of
the early twentieth century may be studied, in all their
process of development, in the long series of Mr. Wells's
prophetic books. Our notions of the future have something of that significance which Freud attributes to our
dreams. And not our notions of the future only: our
notions of the past as well. For if prophecy is an expression of our contemporary fears and wishes, so too,
to a very great extent, is history—or at least what passes
for history among the mass of ordinary unprofessional
folk. Utopias, earthly paradises and earthly hells are
flowers of the imagination which contrive to blossom
and luxuriate even in the midst of the stoniest dates and
documents, even within the fixed and narrow boundaries of established fact. The works of St. Thomas survive; we have a record of the acts of Innocent III. But
that does not prevent our pictures of the Middles Ages

from being as various and as highly coloured as our
pictures of Utopia, the Servile State or the New Jerusalem. We see the past through the refractive medium
of our prejudices, our tastes, our contemporary fears
and hopes. The facts of history exist; but they hardly
trouble us. We select and interpret our documents till
they square with our theories.

The eighteenth century is a period which has been
interpreted and reinterpreted in the most surprisingly
various ways: by its own philosophers (for the eighteenth century was highly self-conscious) as the age of
reason and enlightenment; by the Romantics and their
strange heirs, the Reactionaries and the Early Victo-
rians, as the age of vice and spiritual drought; by the
later nineteenth-century sceptics, who curiously combined the strictest Protestant morality with the most
dogmatically anti-Christian philosophy, as an age of
reason indeed, but of more than dubious character; by
the Beardsleyites of the 'nineties, as an epoch of deliciously depraved frivolity, of futile and therefore
truly aesthetic elegance. The popular conception of the
eighteenth century at the present day is a mixture of
Beardsley's and Voltaire's. We find its morals and its
manners in the highest degree "amusing"; and when we
want a stick to beat the corpses of the Eminent Victo-
rians we apply to Hume or Gibbon, to Voltaire or Helvétius, to Horace Walpole or Madame du Deffand. For
the simpler-minded among us, the eighteenth century

is summed up by Mr. Nigel Playfair's version of *The Beggar's Opera*. The more sophisticated find their *dix-huitième* in the original French documents (judiciously selected) or in the ironic pages of Mr. Lytton Strachey.

Charming historical Utopia! A moment's thought, however, is sufficient to show how arbitrarily we have abstracted it from reality. For who, after all, were the most important, the most durable and influential men that the century produced? The names of Bach, Handel and Mozart present themselves immediately to the mind; of Swedenborg and Wesley and Blake; of Dr. Johnson, Bishop Berkeley and Kant. Of none of these can it be said that he fits very easily into the scheme of *The Beggar's Opera*. True, our pianists and conductors have tried, Procrustes-like, to squeeze the musicians into the *dix-huitième* mould. They play Bach mechanically, Handel lightly, Mozart frivolously, without feeling and therefore without sense, and call the process a "classical" interpretation. But let that pass. The fact remains that the greatest men of the eighteenth century are not in the least what we should call *dix-huitième*.

It must not be imagined, however, that our particular "eighteenth century" is completely mythical. Something like it did genuinely exist, during a couple of generations, among a small class of people in most European countries, especially France. The fact that we have chosen to recreate a whole historical epoch in the image of this intellectually free and morally licentious *dix-huitième* throws some light on our own problems, our own twentieth-century bugbears, our own desires. For a certain section of contemporary society the terms "modern" and "eighteenth century" are almost synonymous. Like our ancestors, we too are in revolt against intellectual authority and moral "prejudices." Perhaps the chief difference between them and us is that they believed in pure reason as well as extra-conjugal love; we Bergsonians do not.

One of the most characteristic representatives of this particular *dix-huitième* which we have chosen to exalt at the expense of all the other possible eighteenth centuries is Crébillon the Younger. We find in his novels all the qualities which we regard as typical of the period: elegance, frivolity, a complete absence of moral "prejudices," especially on the subject of love, a certain dry spirit of detachment and analysis. *Le Sopha* and *La Nuit et le Moment* are documents which, taken by themselves, completely justify our current conception of the age in which they were written. For that reason alone they deserve to be read. One should always be prepared to quote authorities in support of one's theories. Moreover, they are worth reading for their own sakes. For Crébillon was a psychologist and, in his own limited field, one of the most acute of his age.

The typically modern method of presenting character differs from that employed by the novelists of the eighteenth century. In our novels we offer the facts in a so-to-speak raw state, leaving the reader to draw his own conclusions from them. The older psychologists treated the facts to a preliminary process of intellectual digestion; they gave their readers something more than the mere behaviouristic material on which psychological judgments are based; they gave them the conclusions they themselves had already drawn from the facts. Compare Constant's *Adolphe* with the *Ulysses* of James Joyce; the difference of method is manifest. Crébillon is a characteristic eighteenth-century psychologist. With the dry intellectual precision of his age, he describes and comments on his characters, analyses their behaviour, draws conclusions, formulates generalizations. What a contemporary novelist would imply in twenty pages of description and talk, he expresses outright in two or three sentences that are an intellectual summing up of all the evidence. The novelist who employs the older method gains in definition and clarity what he loses in realism, in life, in expansive implication and suggestion. There is much to be said for both methods of presentation; most of all, perhaps, for a combination of the two.

So much for Crébillon's method of presenting character. It is time to consider the sort of people and the particular aspect of their characters which he liked to present. His heroes and heroines are the men and women of our own favourite *dix-huitième*—the eighteenth century whose representative man is rather Casa-

[142]

nova than Bach, rather the Cardinal de Bernis than
Wesley. They are aristocrats who fill their indefinite
leisure with an amateur's interest in literature, art, and
even science (see, for the scientific interests, Cléandre's
story, in *La Nuit et le Moment,* of his physico-physio-
logical argument with Julie) ; with talk and social intercourse, with gambling and country sports; and above
all, with that most perfect of time-killers, *l'amour.* Crébillon's main, his almost exclusive preoccupation is
with the last of these aristocratic amusements. And it
is on his psychology of love—of a certain kind of love—
that his claim to literary immortality must be based.

Crébillon's special province is that obscure border-
land between soul and body, where physiology and psychology meet and mingle and are reciprocally complicated. It is a province of which, during the last century
and in this country, at any rate, we have heard but the
scantiest accounts. It was only with birth that physiology ever made its entrance into the Victorian novel,
not with conception. In these matters, Crébillon's age
was more scientific. The existence of physiology was
frankly admitted at every stage of the reproductive
process. It was mentioned in connection with every
kind of love, from *l'amour passion* to *l'amour goût.* It
was freely discussed, and its phenomena described,
classified and explained. The relations between the
senses and the imagination, between love and pleasure,
between desire and the affections are methodically de-

[143]

fined in that literature of which Crébillon's stories are representative. And it is very right that they should be so defined. For no analysis of love can claim to be complete which ignores the physiological basis and accompaniment of the passion. Love, says Donne in his nearest approach to a versified epigram,

> Love's not so pure and abstract as they use
> To say, who have no mistress but their Muse.

The distinction between sacred and profane, spiritual and fleshly love is an arbitrary, gratuitous and metaphysical distinction. The most spiritual love is rooted in the flesh; the most sacred is only profane love sublimated and refined. To ignore these obvious facts is foolish and slightly dishonest. And indeed, they never have been ignored except by the psychologists of the nineteenth century. The writers of every other age have always admitted them. It was in aristocratic France, however, and during the eighteenth century, that they were most closely and accurately studied. Crébillon *fils* is one of the acutest, one of the most scientific of the students.

Scientific—I apply the epithet deliberately, not vaguely and at random. For Crébillon's attitude towards the phenomena of sex seems to me precisely that of the true scientific investigator. It is with a mind entirely open and unbiassed that he approaches the subject. He contrives to forget that love is a matter of the

[144]

most intimate human concern, that it has been from time immemorial the subject of philosophical speculation and moral precept. Making a clean sweep of all the prejudices, he sets to work, coolly and with detachment, as though the subject of his investigations were something as remote, as utterly divorced from good and evil, as spiral nebulae, liver flukes or the aurora borealis.

Men have always tended to attribute to the objects of their intense emotions, and even to the emotions themselves, some kind of cosmical significance. Mystics and lovers, for example, have never been content to find the justification for their feelings in the feelings themselves: they have asked us to believe that these feelings possess a universal truth value as well as, for themselves, a personal behaviour value. And they have invented cosmogonies and metaphysical systems to justify and explain their emotional attitudes. The fact that all these metaphysical systems are, scientifically speaking, almost certainly untrue in no way affects the value for the individual and for whole societies of the emotions and attitudes which gave them birth. Thus, mysticism will always be a beautiful and precious thing, even though it should be conclusively proved that all the philosophical systems based upon it are nonsensical. And one can be convinced of the superiority of spiritual to carnal, of "conjugial" to "scortatory" love without believing a word of Plato or Swedenborg.

[145]

In a quiet and entirely unpretentious way Crébillon was an expounder of the scientific truth about love—that its basis is physiological; that the intense and beautiful emotions which it arouses cannot be philosophically justified or explained, but should be gratefully accepted for what they are: feelings significant in themselves and of the highest practical importance for those who experience them. He is no vulgar and stupid cynic who denies the existence, because he cannot accept the current metaphysical explanation, of any feelings higher than the merely physical. "Les plaisirs gagnent toujours à être ennoblis," says Crébillon, through the mouth of the Duke in *Le Hasard au Coin du Feu*. It is the man of science who speaks, the unprejudiced observer, the accepter of facts. Pleasure is a fact; so is nobility. He admits the existence of both. Pleasure gains by being ennobled: that is the practical, experimental justification of all the high, aspiring, seemingly infinite emotions evoked by love. True, it may be objected that Crébillon gives too little space in his analysis of love to that which ennobles pleasure and too much to pleasure pure and simple. He would have been more truly scientific if he had reversed the balance; for that which ennobles is of more practical significance, both to individuals and to societies, than that which is ennobled. We may excuse him, perhaps, by supposing that, in the society in which he lived (the Pompadour was his patroness), his opportunities for observing the ennobling passions were scarce in comparison with his opportunities for observing the raw physiological material on which such passions work.

But it is foolish as well as ungrateful to criticize an author for what he has failed to achieve. The reader's business is with what the writer has done, not with what he has left undone. And Crébillon, after all, did do something which, whatever its limitations, was worth doing. What writer, for example, has spoken more acutely on the somewhat scabrous, but none the less important subject of feminine "temperament"? I cannot do better than quote a specimen of his analysis, with the generalization he draws from it. He is speaking here of a woman whose imagination is more ardent than her senses, and who, living in a society where this imagination is perpetually being fired, is for ever desperately trying to experience the pleasures of which she dreams. "Elle a l'imagination fort vive et fort déréglée, et quoique l'inutilité des épreuves qu'elle a faites en certain genre eût dû la corriger d'en faire, elle ne veut pas se persuader qu'elle soit née plus malheureuse qu'elle croit que d'autres ne le sont, et elle se flatte toujours qu'il est réservé au dernier qu'elle prend de la rendre aussi sensible qu'elle désire de l'être. Je ne doute même pas que cette idée ne soit la source de ses déréglements et de la peine qu'elle prend de jouer ce qu'elle ne sent pas. . . . Je dirai plus, c'est qu'aujourd'hui il est prouvé que ce sont les femmes

[147]

à qui les plaisirs de l'amour sont les moins nécessaires qui les recherchent avec la plus de fureur, et que les trois quarts de celles qui se sont perdues avaient reçu de la nature tout ce qu'il leur fallait pour ne l'être pas." Admirable description of a type not at all uncommon in all societies where love-making is regarded as the proper study of womankind! The type, I repeat, is not uncommon; but Crébillon's succinct and accurate description of it is something almost unique.

Here is another passage in which he analyses the motives of a different type of cold woman—a much more dangerous type, it may be remarked: the type to which all successful adventuresses belong. "Soit caprice, soit vanité, la chose du monde qui lui plaît le plus est d'inspirer de désirs; elle jouit du moins des transports de son amant. D'ailleurs, la froideur de ses sens n'empêche pas sa tête de s'animer, et si la nature lui a refusé ce que l'on appelle *le plaisir*, elle lui a en échange donné une sorte de volupté qui n'existe, à la vérité, que dans ses idées; mais qui lui fait peut-être éprouver quelque chose de plus délicat que ce qui ne part que des sens. Pour vous," adds Clitandre, addressing his companion, "pour vous, plus heureuse qu'elle, vous avez, si je ne me trompe, rassemblé les deux."

It would be possible to compile out of the works of Crébillon a whole collection of such character-sketches and aphorisms. "What every Young Don Juan ought to Know" might serve as title to this florilegium. It should be placed in the hands of all those, women as well as men, who propose to lead, professionally, the arduous and difficult life of leisure. Here are a few of the aphorisms which will deserve to find a place in this anthology of psychological wisdom.

"Une jolie femme dépend bien moins d'elle-même que des circonstances; et par malheur il s'en trouve tant, de si peu prévues, de si pressantes, qu'il n'y a point à s'étonner si, après plusieurs aventures, elle n'a connu ni l'amour, ni son cœur. Il s'ensuit que ce qu'on croit la dernière fantaisie d'une femme est bien souvent sa première passion."

"Les sens ont aussi leur délicatesse; à un certain point on les émeut; qu'on le passe, on les révolte."

"L'on n'occupe pas longtemps l'imagination d'une femme sans aller jusqu'à son cœur, ou du moins sans que par les effets cela ne revienne au même."

Of Crébillon's life there is but little to say. It was quite uneventful. The record of it, singularly scanty, contains almost no unusual or surprising element. It was precisely the life which you would expect the author of *Le Sopha* to have led: a cheerful, social, literary life in the Paris of Louis XV. Crébillon was born on St. Valentine's Day, 1707, thus achieving legitimacy by fifteen days; for his parents were only married on the thirty-first of January. His father was Prosper Jolyot de Crébillon, the tragic poet who provoked the envy and the competitive rivalry of Voltaire. I am not ashamed to say that I have never read a line of the elder Crébillon's works. Life is not so long that one can afford to spend even the briefest time in the perusal of eighteenth-century French tragedians.

The literary career of the younger Crébillon began in the theatre. In association with the actors Romagnesi, Biancolelli and Riccoboni he composed a number of satirical pieces and parodies for the Italian comedians. It was at this period that he confided to Sébastien Mercier, "qu'il n'avait encore achevé la lecture des tragédies de son père, mais que cela viendrait. Il regardait la tragédie française comme la farce la plus complète qu'ait pu inventer l'esprit humain."

His first successful novel, *Tanzai et Néardarné, Histoire Japonaise,* was published in 1734. It was so successful, indeed, and so Japanese, that Crébillon, accused of satirizing the Cardinal de Rohan and other important persons, was arrested and thrown into prison, from which, however, the good graces of a royal reader soon released him.

Tanzai was followed in 1736 by *Les Égarements du Cœur et de l'Esprit,* and in 1740 by *Le Sopha.* It was the epoch of Crébillon's social triumphs. He was for some time perpetual chairman of the famous dinners of the Caveau, and there were many other societies of which he was, officially or unofficially, the leading light.

In 1748 he married—somewhat tardily, for he had had a child by her two years before—an English wife,

Lady Mary Howard. It is said that the poor lady squinted, was very ugly, awkward in society, shy and deeply religious. Crébillon seems, none the less, to have been a model husband, while the marriage lasted; which was not very long, however, for Lady Mary died about 1756. Their only child died in infancy a short time after being legitimated.

It was in 1759 that the favour of Madame de Pompadour procured for Crébillon the post of Royal Censor of Literature. He performed his duties conscientiously and to the satisfaction of all parties concerned. On the death of his father, in 1762, he received a pension. In 1774 he became Police Censor as well as Royal Censor. In 1777 he died. For all practical purposes, however, he had been dead fifteen years or more. "Il y a longtemps," said his obituarist, "très longtemps même, qu'il avait eu le chagrin de se voir survivre à lui-même." Melancholy fate! It caused his contemporaries to do him, towards the end, something less than justice. The most enthusiastic of his epitaphs is cool enough:

> Dans ce tombeau gît Crébillon.
> Qui? le fameux tragique?— Non!
> Celui qui le mieux peignit l'âme
> Du petit-maître et de la femme.

The praise is faint. It is meant, perhaps, to damn. But it does not succeed in damning. To have been the best painter of anybody's soul, even the fop's, even the eighteenth-century lady's, is a fine achievement. "Je fus étonnée," says one of Crébillon's characters, describing the charms of her lover's conversation, "je fus étonnée de la sorte de consistance que les objets les plus frivoles semblaient prendre entre ses mains." The whole merit of that French eighteenth century, of which Crébillon was the representative man, consisted precisely in giving "a sort of consistency to the most frivolous objects." To lead a life of leisure gracefully is an art, and though we can all do nothing, few of us contrive to do it well. It is scarcely possible to imagine a life more hopelessly futile than that which was led by the men and women of the old French aristocracy. Intrinsically, such a life seems ghastly in its emptiness and sterility. And yet, somehow, by sheer force of style, these frivolous creatures of the *dix-huitième* contrived to fill the emptiness, to coax the most charming and elegant flowers from the sterility of their existence. To the most futile of lives they gave "a sort of consistency"; they endowed nothingness with solidity and form. Crébillon shared this power with his contemporaries. The conquests of the *petit maître*, the prompt surrenders of Célie and Cidalise and Julie—these are his theme. It seems unpromising in its smallness and its triviality. But by dint of treating it seriously—with the double seriousness of the scientific observer and the literary artist—he has made out of it something which we in our turn are compelled to take seriously. Like Célie, we are astonished.

Justifications

WELL beaten by the Don, Masetto lies groaning in the darkness. To him comes Zerlina, repentantly tender. Kneeling beside him, *"Vedrai, carino,"* she promises in a melody of the most ravishing elegance,

> *Vedrai, carino,*
> *se sei buonino,*
> *che bel rimedio*
>   *ti voglio dar.*
> *È naturale,*
> *non da disgusto,*
> *e lo speziale*
>   *non lo sa far.*
> *È un certo balsamo*
> *che porto adosso.*
> *Dare te'l posso,*
>   *se il vuoi provar.*

And after half a dozen repetitions of *tocca mi qua, qua* and twenty bars of deliciously melodious twiddles, the orchestra ends up, *pianissimo,* but how definitely and satisfyingly! with the chord of C major, and the newly married lovers retire to enjoy their bliss.

È naturale, non da disgusto . . . Da Ponte evidently spoke for himself. This is his description of the manner in which the libretto of *Don Giovanni* was composed: "I sat down at my writing-table and stayed there for

[153]

twelve hours on end, with a little bottle of Tokay on my right hand, an inkstand in the middle, and a box of Seville tobacco on the left. A beautiful young girl of sixteen was living in my house with her mother, who looked after the household. (I should have wished to love her only as a daughter—but . . .) She came into my room whenever I rang the bell, which in truth was fairly often, and particularly when my inspiration seemed to begin to cool. She brought me now a biscuit, now a cup of coffee, or again nothing but her own lovely face, always gay, always smiling, and made precisely to inspire poetic fancy and brilliant ideas." It is a scene from a *settecento* Earthly Paradise—before the Fall of 1789. The mind is its own place, and there have always been plenty of men and women whose home was Da Ponte's Eden. The rest of us are not so fortunate. In the world we inhabit, that *certo balsamo* which Zerlina and her young friends carry about with them is listed as one of the dangerous drugs. Its administration is not permitted, except under a medical certificate. In the moral pharmacopœias of all civilized countries it is official in only one form—matrimony. Made up in this way the *bel rimedio* is "a remedy against sin." Made up in any other way, it *is* sin.

Those who, like Da Ponte, are untroubled in this matter by qualms of conscience, merely ignore the prescriptions of the pharmacopœia. If they want the balm, they take it, in whatever form and from any bootlegger who is willing to supply it. The behaviour of these drug traffickers is so straightforward, their thoughts and feelings so transparently comprehensible, that it is unnecessary to pay any further attention to them. It is just a matter of *tocca mi qua, qua,* and there's an end of it.

But there is another class of men and women, the scrupulous, for whom this simple solution is morally impossible. They want the *certo balsamo* in forms that are not official; they feel impelled to give an unduly violent expression to their lust for power, or social position or money. Current morality condemns these wishes. It would be possible for them, by breaking the law discreetly, to get all they want without discomfort; but they are not prepared even to think of themselves as law-breakers. They reject an enjoyment which is illicit, refuse to be the furtive evaders of a rule of which their own furtiveness tacitly confirms the validity. Declining the dishonourable rôle of bootleggers, they claim to be on the right side of the law, they insist on the essential orthodoxy of their actions. Other people condemn them; they retort by inventing philosophies to prove that they are right.

Many people carry scrupulousness a stage further. There is no question of their committing an act that has been pronounced illegal or immoral. They take their *certo balsamo* as prescribed; they indulge their avarice and their lust for power only in such ways as convention regards as respectable. But all sensualities and egotisms are essentially irrational; and, along with their animal cravings, men feel a hunger and thirst for explanation, for reasonableness, for righteousness. Even a licit indulgence in the irrational can be distressing to the scrupulous. Law and the local system of morality may pronounce such indulgences to be harmless; but they feel it necessary to invent more elaborate justifications of their own.

A complete history of justifications would be, to a great extent, identical with a history of thought. Most political, ethical and even cosmological systems have been essentially justificatory. They are the work either of men in rebellion against the existing system, or of the scrupulous, or of the defenders of orthodoxy.

To be effective, justifications have to be made in terms of the philosophy which condemns the acts or thoughts that it is desired to justify. The scrupulous are concerned to prove that the irrational they so much dread is in truth rational or even divine; the rebels, that they are really, if the matter be examined with an unprejudiced eye, more Catholic than the Pope and more royalist than the King. Conversely, the supporters of an established system will try to show that they have on their side, not only tradition and divine revelation, but also logic and considerations of utility.

An elaborate system of justification often does more than it was intended to do. In justifying one set of thoughts, impulses and actions, the author finds (or his readers find) that he is logically committed to believing in the rightness of other doings and other feelings, which he had not originally thought of justifying. Thus, a system intended originally to justify simple fornication may turn out to be logically capable of justifying murder. Those who want to commit murder will seize on the excuse offered by the system, and even those who don't will find themselves impelled by the force of logic into this course.

Philosophies are devices for making it possible to do, coolly, continuously and with a good conscience, things which otherwise one could do only in the heat of passion, spasmodically and under the threat of subsequent remorse. Unsophisticated by thought, anger soon dies down; but supply a man with a philosophy proving that he is right to be angry, and he will go on performing in cold blood the acts of malice which otherwise he could have performed only when the fit was upon him. Philosophies, which their authors devised in order to justify some relatively harmless craving, have been subsequently made the excuse for monstrous iniquities. For example, the seventeenth-century Puritans were anxious to prove that there was no incompatibility between trade and wealth on the one hand and Christian virtues on the other. The philosophy which they concocted out of the Old Testament did much more than it was meant to do. Not only did it prove that rich nonconformist merchants were thoroughly virtuous; it also proved that workmen, peasants and, in general, all the poor were thoroughly vicious, therefore that they deserved all the miseries they suffered, and a good many more as well. The surprising thing about the industrial revolution is not that capitalists and *entrepreneurs* should have behaved badly; it is that they should have been so serenely convinced of their perfect goodness. For this the philosophy of the Puritans, reinforced at a later period by that of the political economists, was responsible.

In the pages which follow, I shall illustrate these general remarks on justication by a few concrete examples chosen almost at random from the illimitable literature of the subject. The choice has been determined more by the hazards of my recent reading than by anything else. My only guiding principle has been that the examples should be curious, striking and even, in certain cases, extravagant. It is by studying madness that psychologists have learnt to understand the workings of the healthy mind. Similarly, it is in the most absurd and fantastic instances that the mechanism of the essentially normal and commonplace process of justification is seen most clearly at work. If my principal examples are concerned with the *certo balsamo*, it is because the theological and philosophical devices which have been invented for the justification of sexual activity, whether licit or illicit, have generally been more fantastic and far-fetched than those by which men have sought to

[158]

moralize their swindles and murders, their cruelties and rapacities, the manifestations of their vanity, pride and personal ambition.

My first examples belong to the class of justifications by religious experience. Such justifications tend to be especially extravagant where the prevailing theological system is one which postulates the reality of guidance by a personal God. For men and women brought up in such a system, it is easy to justify any action by identifying the desire to perform it with the direct prompting of the deity. In certain of these theological systems, God is regarded as completely transcendent and of a nature utterly incommensurable with man's. This being so, He becomes capable of anything; we must not be surprised to find God guiding us to perform acts which would be judged, by merely human standards, as crimes and lunacies.

Kierkegaard wrote a whole book on this subject, choosing as his theme the story of Abraham and Isaac. The command to sacrifice Isaac was, he insists, genuinely divine. God's ways are so emphatically not ours that there is no cause for astonishment in His ordering His servant to commit a crime. Such "temporary suspensions of the moral order" are proofs of God's omnipotence and transcendence. Kierkegaard's choice of an example is significant. His God is a justifier of cruelty, not of sensuality. The idea that there could be a temporary suspension of the laws of sexual morality is evidently repugnant to him. That God should prompt to murder is, to his mind, more easily conceivable than that He should prompt to an act of sexual indulgence. Kierkegaard's attitude is widely shared at the present day. There are plenty of pious churchmen who consider that God approves of men killing their fellows in war, but who would be horrified at the suggestion that fornication and adultery can ever be anything but detestable in His eyes. Those who invoke guidance to justify behaviour commonly regarded as immoral may be grouped in two main classes. In the first class we place those whom Dante would have consigned to the lower circles of hell—the violent and malicious; in the second we place the merely incontinent whose chief preoccupation is with the *certo balsamo* and who find themselves divinely guided towards sexual promiscuity. The two classes cannot in practice be sharply distinguished. Those who are guided towards promiscuity may also be guided, as we shall see, towards pride, fraud and violence.

In choosing the sacrifice of Isaac as his example, Kierkegaard displayed a certain timidity. For after all, this particular suspicion of the moral order was not complete; the angel and that eleventh-hour ram saved Isaac from the knife. If he had really had the courage of his convictions, Kierkegaard would have chosen a case like that of Thomas Schucker, the Swiss Anabaptist who, in 1527, cut off his brother's head. "He called together a numerous assembly and declared to the company that he perceived himself under the influence of the spirit of God. Upon which he commanded his brother to kneel down, and took a sword. His father and mother and some others demanded what he was about to do. *Be satisfied,* replied he, *I will do nothing but what is revealed to me by our heavenly father.* The company waited impatiently for the event, when they saw him draw his sword and cut off his brother's head. He was punished by the magistrates as his crime deserved; but he showed no signs of repentance, and declared upon the scaffold that he had executed the orders of God." The most remarkable feature of this story is not that Schucker should have felt himself guided to cut off his brother's head; it is that the brother should have consented to let his head be cut off and that the numerous assembly should have looked on without a protest. Under the influence of his religion and justified by its theology, Schucker was merely taking too seriously a childish fantasy of murder. But the victim and the spectators had no such fantasies; if they behaved in the way they did, it was because it seemed to them inherently probable that Schucker's revelation was valid.

Those who believe that God gives guidance are forced to admit that what *feels* like a divine command is in fact very often a prompting from some all too human source. Accordingly they advise anyone who receives what seems a guidance to confide it to others and ask their opinion upon it. A guidance that can stand up to the criticism of a group may be relied upon as being of divine origin. Thomas Schucker's guidance came through this test with flying colours. We must either believe that an act of criminal imbecility can be divinely inspired, or that the test is far from infallible. The case of Thomas Schucker is not unique; it is merely a particularly extravagant specimen of a very common type of religious aberration. A group under supposedly divine guidance is not quite so frequently the victim of absurd fantasies and disreputable desires as is an individual; but the difference is merely one of degree, not of kind. There is no dogma so queer, no behaviour so eccentric or even outrageous, but a group of people can be found to think it divinely inspired.

Here, for example, is the case, chosen from among a thousand others, of the Reverend Henry James Prince and his disciples. Prince was born in 1811 in the West Country; was articled to a doctor; then, at twenty-six, decided to take Orders. A journal which he kept at this period was published in 1859 for the edification of his followers. It is a typical specimen of evangelical literature. One opens it at random upon such entries as this, for September 20th, 1835: "In the evening I found strength to expound John iii. with boldness to a party of Mr. M. C.'s and then to pray with them. Afterwards spoke seriously to F. H., endeavouring to convince him

that he needed a new heart. At night was assaulted
with a severe trial, when I found it exceedingly difficult to resist the idolatrous feeling of self-complacency
on account of those doings." A month later he "dined
at Dr. H.'s and spent a rational evening. He lent me
Bickersteth's Guide to Prophecy, and gave me a book
by Mr. Cunningham on the Millennium." On May
17th, 1837, "Jesus vouchsafed after dinner to visit my
soul with His love; it was quite delicious to my poor
barren soul; my heart melted over the dying Lamb, and
the sight of His bleeding love was such that for a season my soul seemed quite swallowed up in the enjoyment of His dying love; I felt that I had done the
bloody deed, and loathed myself; all that I could do
was to sigh and weep and look and love."

In the following spring Prince entered St. David's
College, at Lampeter, to prepare for ordination. He was
an exemplary student—too exemplary, indeed, for the
taste of most of his fellows, who resented the zeal for
self-improvement displayed by Prince and a small band
of earnest companions. One of these companions, Arthur Augustus Rees, published in 1846 a pamphlet,
*The Rise and Progress of the Heresy of the Rev. H. J.
Prince,* which contains an account of the young man's
career at Lampeter. It was, so it seems, the reading of
a book called *The Life and Writings of Gerhard Tersteegen* (Tersteegen was a German pietist of the eighteenth century) that launched young Prince upon the

course that was to lead him to the Agapemone. Tersteegen convinced him of the importance of living
always under guidance; so much so, that "at length he
was determined to say or do nothing without a previous
intimation of the divine mind. For example, if Mr. P.
were about to take a walk and there were every appearance of rain, he would not carry out his umbrella without first asking the will of God." In due course, he came
to believe that he could always discover what the will
of God really was: an infallible intuition revealed it in
every conjunction of life. Judged by ordinary standards,
God's advice might often seem rather injudicious; but
since it was God's it was right. Prince would always act
upon it, even in defiance of his judgment.

The will of God had a good deal to do with Prince's
two marriages. The first, contracted while still a student at Lampeter, was with a Miss Martha Freeman.
This lady was old enough to be her husband's mother,
but possessed by way of compensation an independent
income. A friend of Prince's family, she had contrib-
uted towards the expenses of the young man's education. In return he converted her from Catholicism to
Anglicanism, and had acted almost from boyhood as
her spiritual adviser. Their relationship was simultaneously that of husband and wife, mother and son,
spiritual father and daughter. Alas! the couple had
little time to enjoy this complicated bliss; a few months
only after Prince's ordination to the curacy of Char-

linch, in Somerset, the poor old lady died. Whereupon, with a haste which his friends could only regard as indecent, but which he himself explained as being due to the will of God, he married Miss Julia Starky, sister of the rector of the parish.

Mr. Starky was Prince's senior by some years; but from the first his relations to his new curate were those of disciple to master. Prince, it is evident, was one of those born snake-charmers and lion-tamers who go through life effortlessly dominating their fellow-men and women. Such magnetism is a dangerous gift, which it is almost impossible not to abuse or be abused by. Prince duly succumbed to the temptations into which his own powers led him; he fascinated others into believing him a superior being; feasted his self-esteem on their adulation until it swelled to monstrous proportions; then invoked the Almighty to justify his pretensions and to moralize his sexual eccentricities.

In *The Charlinch Revival,* which he published in 1842 (in order, "under the Divine blessing, to stir up the hearts of the Lord's people"), Prince reveals himself to us at the moment when he first discovered the full extent of his powers. Charlinch was an agricultural parish, peopled by stolid Saxon rustics, in whom the temperature of religious zeal was little, if at all, above absolute zero. The revival began in October 1841. Mr. Prince, who had for some time been "shut up" and deprived of his ordinary power to preach a stirring ser-

[165]

mon, found himself suddenly inspired. There was a memorable Sunday afternoon when "the church was unusually full, but the minister felt as if he had nothing to say; he was still shut up. In the pulpit, however, the spirit of prayer came on him and he prayed for twenty minutes with considerable unction. He then told his congregation that he would read the text to them, Ephesians v. 14, and that if the Lord were pleased to speak by him He would; and if not, that he must hold his tongue, as he could not speak from himself. He had scarcely spoken these words, when the Spirit came upon him with power: certainly *he* did not preach, but the Holy Ghost preached by him. The word was not vehement, and far too solemn to be violent; but it was searching like fire, heavy as a hammer, and sharper than a two-edged sword." The congregation was overwhelmed. "Several men and women sobbed aloud; the head of most dropped on their breast, the hearts of all were awestruck. (One boy excepted.)" Galvanized, the parish started out of its secular repose. The revival had begun.

Prince's next great victory was won in the Sunday School, where he "had laboured fourteen months without witnessing so much as *one* child become even serious." On December 10th, 1841, about fifty children were assembled in the Charlinch school. "In a few minutes, the Holy Ghost came upon the minister with the most tremendous power. . . . About twenty of the

[166]

children were pierced to the heart by it, and appeared to be in great distress; but the bigger boys continued unmoved, and some of them even seemed disposed to laugh. In a short time, however, the word reached *them* too, and they were smitten to the heart with a most dreadful conviction of their sin and danger. . . . In about ten minutes the spectacle presented by the school-room was truly awful; out of fifty children present there were not so many as *ten* that *could stand upright*. Boys and girls, great and small together, were either leaning against the wall quite overcome by their feelings of distress, or else bowed down with their faces hidden in their hands, and sobbing in the severest agony." The triumph was complete. "Who can possibly resist the conviction that the hand of the Lord hath done this?" Certainly not the Reverend Henry James Prince.

The revivalists were so excessively zealous that, in May 1842, the Bishop of Bath and Wells revoked Mr. Prince's licence to preach. Charlinch was becoming too hot to hold its curate. He migrated; but a similar fate overtook him in two other parishes. Finally, "after some months waiting on God for guidance in faith and prayer," he left the Established Church and started to preach on his own—at Brighton, where he founded an Adullam Chapel; at Weymouth, where Mr. Starky, who had also had a difference with the Bishop, was minis-tering to a considerable flock of Starkyites; at Spaxton,

[167]

a village near Charlinch and the site of the future Agapemone.

The heroes of tragedy are torn between love and honour—in other words, between egoism and egotism, between craving and pride, between the urge to indulge oneself and the urge to dominate others. In Prince there was no conflict. The two motives presented themselves not simultaneously but in succession. He began with the pursuit of honour and, having achieved it, went on to love. His first systematic efforts at justification were made on behalf of his ambition and vanity; it was not till later that he used his theology and his religious experiences for moralizing his sensualities.

It was in the spring of 1849 that he wrote to his friend Rees to inform him that the Holy Ghost had taken up its residence within himself; and by the end of the same year he had evolved a complete system of theology, based firmly upon the foundation of unquestionable experience: the experience of his identity with the spirit of God. This theology subsequently underwent certain modifications under the pressure of his desires. As the claims of sensuality became more insistent, new theological dogmas had to be invented to justify them. In 1843 pride and vanity were in the ascendant, and the refinements of the doctrine elaborated twelve years later in *The Little Book Open*—refinements intended to sanctify Prince's cravings for the *certo balsamo*—had not yet been invented. The fully developed doctrine will be described in due course. Meanwhile, we must see how Brother Prince, as he now called himself, was guided to deal with the important problem of finance. His methods were simplicity itself. Disciples would come down to breakfast to find a note couched in some such words as these: "The Lord hath need of £50 to be used for a special purpose unto His glory. The spirit would have this known unto you. Amen." So great was the faith of those to whom such communications were addressed that they would sit down at once to draw the cheque. So far so good. But it soon became clear that what the Lord really needed was capital—a good solid lump of it. And in due course the capital appeared. Here is the story of the first twenty thousand.

After being deprived of his curacy at Charlinch, Prince spent some months as curate of Stoke, in Suffolk. Here he made the acquaintance of Mr. and Mrs. Nottidge, and their four unmarried daughters. These ladies, who were no longer in their first youth, became Prince's disciples and, when he left Stoke (under orders, this time, from the Bishop of Ely), followed him to Brighton and subsequently into the west of England. In 1844, Mr. Nottidge died, leaving each of his daughters about six thousand pounds. Shortly afterwards God intimated to Brother Prince that it was His will that three of the Miss Nottidges, Agnes, Harriet and Clara, should marry three of Prince's followers, George

Thomas, Lewis Price and William Cobbe, respectively. The ladies hesitated for a moment, then decided that the will of God must be obeyed, and the three marriages were celebrated simultaneously, at Swansea, on July 9th, 1845. In the following year Agnes parted from her husband—not, however, before parting with her six thousand pounds, which had been made over on her marriage to Mr. Thomas, who in his turn had made them over (for such was the will of God) to Brother Prince. The Cobbes and Prices did likewise. These gifts, to which were added a thousand pounds from Starky, and no less than ten thousand from a Mr. Malin and four Miss Malins, formed the nucleus of a considerable fortune which was afterwards invested in the purchase and maintenance of the Agapemone.

Meanwhile, the fourth Miss Nottidge (aged forty-four and called Louisa) had returned to her mother in Suffolk. Not for long, however. In December 1845 she came at Prince's invitation—or rather, at the invitation of the Holy Ghost—to Weymouth; thence, after some months, migrated to Charlinch. She was living quietly there in a cottage, with Mrs. Prince, when her brother, the Rev. Edmund Nottidge, and her brother-in-law, Frederick Ripley, drove up in a chaise and abducted her. Louisa was taken first of all to her mother's house in London; but on "declaring that Prince was the Almighty in human form, she was, on the 12th of November 1846, upon the usual medical certificate, placed in a private lunatic asylum in Middlesex, where she continued until the 14th of May 1848, when she was discharged by the order of the Lunacy Commissioner." From the asylum, Louisa hurried straight back to Spaxton and, within three days of her release, had transferred the whole of her property to Brother Prince. These six thousand pounds were dearly bought; for their transfer was to lead, twelve years later, to a lawsuit which was a source of much pain to the Spaxton community. Louisa died in 1858, and in 1860 her brother, Ralph Nottidge, filed a suit against Prince in the Court of Chancery, for the return of £5728, 7s. 7d. "In 1848," runs the summary of the case in the *Law Journal Reports,* "a person pretending that he had a divine mission obtained a gift of stock from a lady by imposing a belief on her mind that he sustained a supernatural character. The lady's relations were aware of the gift at the time it was made, and she resided with and was supported by the donee from 1848 up to her death in 1858. Upon a bill by the administrator of the lady, the Court ordered the donee to refund the stock, with interest thereon from the time of her death." And now the point which made the decision worthy of record: "Whether the donee really believed that he was the supernatural being he represented himself to be, was immaterial."

At the time of Louisa's release from her asylum, Nottidge *v.* Prince was still in the distant future. The

present was a season of triumph. Crowds came to listen
to the preaching of the Two Witnesses, as Prince and
Starky called themselves; the number of believers increased; money came pouring in. Brother Prince decided to found a community to be called The Agapemone, or Abode of Love. Two hundred acres of land
were bought at Spaxton, a handsome mansion erected,
gardens laid out. The hothouses were filled with exotic
plants, the stables with magnificent horses, the cellars
with the choicest Madeira and claret. There was a
chapel, complete with stained-glass windows and Gothic
trimmings, but a chapel that was at the same time the
principal drawing-room. It was furnished with arm-
chairs, a comfortable sofa and a billiard-table. To the
sinless and perfected inhabitants of the Agapemone all
activities were holy; a game of snooker was a sacrament
like any other.

Into the Agapemone Brother Prince settled down
with some sixty disciples—gentlefolk and servants. His
state, in these early years, was lordly. He bought the
Queen-Dowager's equipage with four white horses and
drove through the countryside as though he were an
emperor. In London, when he visited the Great Exhibition of 1851, his open carriage was preceded by
outriders, bareheaded, as befitted men in the presence
of the Lord. Letters were sent through the post addressed to "Our Lord God, Spaxton, Somerset," and
were duly delivered. Brother Prince, or "Beloved" as

now he preferred to be called by his followers, had climbed to the pinnacle of Honour. It was time for Love.

At the beginning of the 'fifties a young lady called Miss Paterson had joined the flock. Hepworth Dixon, who visited the Agapemone some years later, has left a description of a certain fascinating "Sister Zoe," whom he identified (though she refused to give her mundane name) with the *ci-devant* Paterson. In a pale, romantic way, Sister Zoe was extremely beautiful. "Guercino might have painted such a girl for one of his rapt and mounting angels." Beloved was smitten. But a man whose soul was the residence of the Holy Ghost—who had indeed, by this time, actually become the Holy Ghost—could hardly be content with a bootlegged *balsamo*. His affair with Zoe had to be justified. He might, of course, have written her a little note to the effect that the Lord had need of her for a special purpose unto His glory. But he must have felt that this would not be enough. Beloved lived in a society which honoured the Low Church mill-owner, growing rich on sweated labour, but was horrified by sexual impropriety. A man might grind the faces of the poor; but so long as he refrained from caressing his neighbours' wives and daughters, he was regarded as virtuous. In money matters Beloved had found plain guidance quite sufficient; but when it came to sensuality, more elaborate justifications were needed. These were set out in

The Little Book Open, published in 1856. After a brief
introduction, the theme of the Little Book is announced in capital letters for all to understand. The
subject of Brother Prince's testimony is "THE RE-
DEMPTION OF THE BODY." The Gospel "ad-
dressed itself to the soul of man. It left out the flesh."
Beloved had appeared to remedy this defect.

The cosmology and theology, in terms of which Mr.
Prince rationalized his desire to have an affair with
Miss Paterson, may be briefly summed up as follows.
God enters periodically into covenants with man,
through chosen individuals. The first covenant was at
the Creation, and Adam was God's witness. The second
was at the Flood, and the witness was Noah. The third
was entered into after the building of the Tower of
Babel; Abraham was the witness on this occasion. The
fourth, with Jesus as witness, at the Redemption upon
the cross. And now, at Spaxton, "God, in Jesus Christ,
has again entered into covenant with man, at the resurrection of mankind, and I am His witness. This one
man, myself, has Jesus Christ selected and appointed
His witness to His counsel and purpose, to conclude the
day of grace and to introduce the day of judgment, to
close the dispensation of the spirit and to enter into
covenant with the FLESH." How sorely the poor flesh
needed this covenant! It had become God's enemy at
the Fall—with an enmity that "neither the holiness of
the law could eradicate, nod the Grace of God amend.

[174]

. . . Even the dying love of a crucified Redeemer never once took away the enmity of the flesh of the believer against God; but rather brought it the more to light." The Gospel had saved only souls, not flesh. Beloved had come to save the flesh. He had already "revealed the mind of the Lord concerning the dispensation of the spirit—the Gospel—by living it as a spiritual body." (I neglected to remark before that Henry James Prince had for some time ceased to exist, and that what people took for the ex-curate of Charlinch was a visible manifestation of the Spirit of God.) Having lived the Gospel in a spiritual body, "he was now to bring to light, or reveal, the mind of the Lord concerning flesh, by living it in flesh. Accordingly there was given unto him a reed like unto a rod; and the angel said, arise and measure the temple of God. He did so."

The circumstances in which he did so were singular in the extreme. He announced to the people in the Agapemone that "it was now God's purpose to extend His love from heaven to earth, from spirit to flesh, from soul to body. . . . Agreeably thereto He (the Holy Ghost) took flesh—a woman. He did this through Brother Prince, as flesh; *yet not Brother Prince as natural flesh* . . . Thus the Holy Ghost took flesh in the person of those whom He had called as flesh. Thus He did measure the temple of God; and the reed like unto a rod wherewith He did measure it was the flesh He had taken." Having thus explained the meaning of his

[175]

symbol, Brother Prince launches into an account of his taking of the flesh. "He took the flesh absolutely in His *sovereign will*. . . . He had no respect for any other will than His own. He was not influenced by what others would think or say. He did not even consult or in any way make known His intention to the flesh He took, until He actually did take it in the presence of others; and then He took it with power and authority, as flesh that belonged to God and was at His absolute disposal; so that in the taking of it He left it no choice of its own. He took it in *free grace*. It was *flesh* He took; flesh that knew not God, that wanted not God, that was ignorant of Him; and, like all other flesh in its nature, contrary to the spirit. He took it as it was—ignorant, indifferent, independent, at enmity against God, and having nothing to commend it to Him. He took it in *love*. Not because it loved Him, for it did not; but because it pleased Him to set His love upon it. And though He took it in absolute power and authority, without consulting its pleasure, or even giving it a choice, yet He took it in love; for having taken it, the manner of His life with it was such as flesh could not but know and appreciate as love.

"Moreover, although it was natural flesh He took, and therefore flesh indifferent to and at enmity with God, He never for a moment made it sensible of this, but in everything and at all times, regarded it and treated it according to His own mind, WHICH WAS

[176]

TO SEE NO EVIL IN IT; in fact, He loved it as His own flesh.

"According to the purpose He had declared, He kept it with Him continually, by day and by night. He took it openly with Him wherever He went, not being ashamed of it; and made its life happy and agreeable by affording it the enjoyment of every simple and innocent gratification."

Through this muddy verbiage, we divine the oddest realities. From Hepworth Dixon, who had sources of information not available at the present time, we learn that the covenant of God (in the person of Mr. Prince) with the flesh (in the person of Miss Paterson) was sealed in a public act of worship, upon the sofa in that consecrated billiard-room at Spaxton. Beloved had announced in advance that the great event was to take place on a given day and at a predetermined hour. What he did not reveal in advance was the name of the particular piece of flesh which was to be reconciled. One can reconstruct the scene: the little congregation sitting in apprehensive expectation round the billiard-table in the chapel; the solemn entry of Beloved; a few prayers offered by the two Anointed Ones, otherwise Messrs. Thomas and Starky; the singing in unison of one of those hymns composed by Beloved in his own honour; then, falling upon the vibrant religious silence, the words of Beloved, announcing the name of the chosen flesh. One can reconstruct the scene, I repeat;

but when it comes to Miss Paterson's thoughts and feelings, imagination boggles. "He took it in love. Not because it loved Him, for it did not; but because it pleased Him to set His love upon it." To set His love upon it, "with power and authority, and in the presence of others." Whether Beloved would have behaved in this extraordinary way if he had been a mere bootlegger of sexual pleasures may be doubted. But in justifying his desires for Miss Paterson, he had created a theology which made the performance in the billiard-room a sacred duty. As plain Mr. Prince, he would never have thought of executing more than a straightforward seduction. As the divine witness of a new dispensation, he was bound to do something spectacular and uncommon. He did it, with a vengeance.

The public initiation in the billiard-room was not the last of Miss Paterson's ordeals. New trials were in store for her; in due course, she became pregnant. Now, according to the Princean theology there was to be no birth under the new dispensation, just as there was to be no death. Beloved and his followers had become immortal and at the same time divinely sterile. In spite of which, it soon became apparent that Sister Zoe was in a family way. For a moment, Beloved was at a loss to understand. Then, from on high, the explanation was vouchsafed. Doomed to annihilation, Satan was making a last despairing effort. Miss Paterson's baby was the result. How it was received when it arrived,

this child of flesh by the Holy Ghost through the instrumentality of the Devil, is not recorded; nor how
it was brought up. Sitting in the billiard-saloon-chapel,
on the very sofa where the covenant had been sealed,
Hepworth Dixon saw a solitary little creature playing
in the garden outside. It is our only glimpse of this
most unwelcome of children.

The case of Nottidge *v.* Prince was heard in 1860—
at a moment, that is to say, when the mid-nineteenth-
century reaction towards rationalism was setting in. It
is a significant fact that, between 1859, the year of the
Irish revival, and 1873, the year of Moody's first visit
to Edinburgh, we have no record of any considerable
outburst of religious excitement in Great Britain. If
the fortunes of the Agapemone began henceforward to
decline, that was not solely due to the strictures of Vice-
Chancellor Stuart; it was also and perhaps mainly due
to the fact that people with money were losing their interest in Covenants and Anointed Ones. If they wanted
justifications for unorthodox behaviour they looked
for them elsewhere than in theology. The chosen band
lived on at Spaxton, steadily shrinking as the immor-
tals who composed it died off, steadily growing poorer
as the value of money declined and the original capital
was eroded away. Beloved lingered on and on, outliving all his original followers, outliving even the age of
rationalism. For in the later 'eighties the tide began to
turn. Intellect went out of fashion. Nietzsche was re-

garded as a great thinker, Bergson had written his first books, and money began to pour once more into the coffers of the Agapemone. A branch was opened at Clapton, where an Ark of the Covenant was built at a cost of nearly twenty thousand pounds. After Beloved's death in 1899, the pastor of the Ark, the Rev. T. H. Smyth Pigott, became Beloved II, and, with a punctuality that bespeaks the unchangeableness of basic human motives, proceeded to repeat all that his predecessor had done. The urge to domination had first to be satisfied and theologically justified; then the craving for the *certo balsamo*. Smyth Pigott did both—becoming God in 1902 and producing, in 1905 and 1908, two illegitimate children called respectively Glory and Power. In due course, he also died. The Agapemone still exists.

Both in doctrine and in practice, Brother Prince was wildly unorthodox. Coventry Patmore's loves were nuptial and his religion Catholic. But, for scrupulous souls, even nuptial love is an odd, inexplicable kind of activity, requiring to be rationalized and sanctified. Patmore found what he required in the ancient doctrine which sees in the consummation of human passion a type and symbol of the union of God with souls and with the Church. The doctrine, I repeat, is old and unorthodox. Patmore's eccentricity consisted in insisting upon its truth with excessive emphasis, in taking too literally an analogy that most writers have preferred to regard as a kind of poetical metaphor. In a prose work, *Sponsa*

[180]

Dei, this literalness of interpretation was pushed, indeed, so far that a clerical friend advised the book's suppression. But the published poems and, above all, the little volume of aphorisms, *The Rod, the Root and the Flower,* make it sufficiently clear what the lost book must have contained.

Patmore suffuses the whole universe, natural as well as supernatural, with sex. "No writer, sacred or profane, ever uses the words 'he' or 'him' of the soul. It is always 'she' or 'her'; so universal is the intuitive knowledge that the soul, with regard to God who is her life, is feminine." (A whole book could be written on the way in which thought has been affected by the accidents of grammar. The word *anima* means the principle of animal life, as opposed to *animus,* which stands for the principle of spiritual life. For some odd reason Christian theologians labelled their particular conception of the soul with the first and less appropriate of these two words. Grammatically, the Latin Christian soul was feminine; what more natural than to suppose that it was in some sort physiologically female? For Greeks the soul might be either feminine or neuter. Either *psyche* or, the word habitually used by St. Paul, *pneuma.* Brought up on *anima,* modern theologians have preferred to this non-committal neuter the personifiable feminine substantive. It is owing to a grammatical prejudice that earnest ladies call themselves psychic rather than pneumatic, and that Coventry Patmore was able to justify his connubial tastes in terms of Catholic theology.)

The soul, then, is a woman; and "woman, according to the *Salve Regina*, is our Life, our Sweetness and our Hope. God is so only in so far as He is 'made flesh,' i.e., Woman. The Flesh of God is the Head of man, says St. Augustine. Thus the Last is indeed the First. 'The lifting of her eyelash is my Lord.' " Again, "Woman is the visible glory of God . . . The Word made Flesh is the Word made Woman." "Heaven becomes very intelligible and attractive when it is discovered to be—Woman."

Feminine, the soul knows her God in a consummated marriage. For "all knowledge worthy of the name is nuptial knowledge." Even death is a form of married love—charged as it is with "a hope intense of kisses close beyond conceit of sense." Mysticism is essentially connubial. "Lovers put out the candle and draw the curtains when they wish to see the god and the goddess; and, in the higher Communion, the night of thought is the light of perception." God is discovered by touch and "the Beatific vision is not seen by the eyes, but is a substance which is sucked as through a nipple." "God Himself becomes a concrete object and an intelligible joy when contemplated as the eternal felicity of a lover with the beloved, the Ante-type and very original of the Love which inspires the poet and the thrush." Conversely, the felicity of the lover with the beloved and the inenarrable experiences of touch are foretastes of the Beatific Vision. "There are some who even in this life can say, 'Under the Tree where my Mother was debauched, Thou has redeemed me.'"

The most distinctive feature of Patmore's doctrine is that which attributes to God a kind of *nostalgie de la boue* and therefore justifies the more god-like among human beings (such, of course, as Patmore himself) in seeking out and cultivating the extremes of sensual irrationality.

"Enough," he makes the woman, Psyche, cry,

> "Enough, enough, ambrosial plumed Boy!
> My bosom is aweary of thy breath.
> Thou kisseth joy to death.
> Have pity of my clay-conceived birth
> And maiden's simple mood,
> Which longs for ether and infinitude,
> As thou, being God, crav'st littleness and earth."

The mystery of the incarnation provides Patmore with an analogy to marital bliss. Addressing himself to the Virgin, he writes as follows:

> Life's cradle and death's tomb!
> To lie within whose womb,
> There, with divine self-will infatuate,
> Love-captive to the thing He did create,
> Thy God did not abhor,
> No more
> Than Man, in Youth's high spousal tide,
> Abhors at last to touch

[183]

The strange lips of his long-procrastinating Bride;
Nay, not the least imagined part as much!
   Ora pro me!

He returns again to the same theme in other poems.
In "The Dream," for example, we read:

> The pride of personality,
> Seeking its highest, aspires to die,
> And in unspeakably profound
> Humiliation, Love is crown'd!
> And from his exaltation still
> Into his ocean of good-will
> He curiously casts the lead
> To find strange depths of lowlihead.

It is, however, in *The Rod, the Root and the Flower*
that the theme is treated most fully. "Spirit craves conjunction with and eternal captivity to that which is not
spirit; and the higher the spirit, the greater the craving. God desires depths of humiliation and contrast of
which man has no idea; so that the stony callousness
and ignorance which we bemoan in ourselves may not
impossibly be an additional cause in Him of desire for
us. . . . Human love requires to be grounded in the
sensitive nature, in order to give counterpoise and reality to its spiritual heights.

"What if the love of God demands even a deeper
foundation in the *un*spiritual and in the junction and
reconcilement of 'the Highest with the Lowest'? There
are obscure longings in the natural man; glimpses of

felicities of an 'Unknown Eros,' which it is perhaps worse than vain to endeavour to indulge; a desire for fruits of the Tree of Knowledge which seem to promise that we 'shall be as Gods,' if we partake of them. Maybe, to such of us as become Gods by participation, these fruits will be found fruits of the Tree of Life, as are other fruits, which, in the eating, have only 'a savour of death unto death,' until they have been refused, in obedience to a temporary prohibition, and only tasted in God's season and with the divine appetite of Grace. Meantime, it is permitted to such as have qualified themselves for such contemplation, to meditate upon the dim glimpse we can catch of such things, as they exist in God, who, as St. Thomas Aquinas teaches, *knows* matter, as he knows all his creation, with love and desire."

What lies behind the veils of this mysterious utterance? We can only obscurely guess.

Odd examples of justifications by guidance and theology could be multiplied indefinitely. There are the refined and aristocratic Muckers in East Prussia, with their ritual of exhibitionism and long-drawn sexual confessions; there are the Perfectionist Bundlers, a sect of American ladies who were guided to burst into clergymen's bedrooms at night; there were the Revivalists, with their spiritual wives—so closely allied in practice, if not in theory, to the Mormons with their all too solid and tangible harems. Or again, one could

[185]

mention the reverend gentleman who boasted that "he could carry a virgin in each hand without the least stir of unholy passion," or the ladies described by Mrs. Whitall Smith in her *Personal Experiences of Fanaticism,* who cultivated the art of giving themselves physical "thrills," under the impression that they were receiving the Baptism of the Spirit. One could mention the early Spiritualists. Here is a statement made by one of them in 1867: "During a year and a half I became very impressible; in fact a medium; the invisible guides impressed me with many ideas of a religious nature. Among other things I became strongly impressed with the incompatibility between myself and my wife; and, on the other hand, with the growing affinity between Mrs. Swain and myself. . . . Nine-tenths of the mediums I ever knew were in this unsettled state, either divorced or living with an affinity. The majority of spiritualists teach Swedenborg's doctrine of *one* affinity, appointed by Providence, for all eternity; although they do not blame people for consorting when there is an attraction; else, how is the affinity to be found? Another class travelled from place to place, finding a great many affinities everywhere."

It would be possible, I repeat, to multiply such instances indefinitely. Possible, but not particularly profitable. The principles of religious justification have been sufficiently illustrated by the few characteristic examples I have given. What follows is an example of philosophical justification—chosen deliberately for its revealing extravagance. The work in question is Laurence Oliphant's *Sympneumata,* published, near the end of its author's life, in 1885. Oliphant's was an oddly variegated career. He was born at Cape Town and brought up in Ceylon. As a young man he visited Nepal and Russia, served as Lord Elgin's secretary at Washington and again, after a visit to Circassia during the Crimean War, in China. In 1861, when he was thirty-two, he was appointed first secretary in Japan; but his diplomatic career was cut short by an attack on the Legation, in which he almost lost his life. He returned to Europe, served as *Times* correspondent in Poland and Holstein, and in the intervals dined out in the best society and wrote successful novels. In 1865 he was elected to Parliament. Three years later he resigned his seat and emigrated to America, to become a member of "the Brotherhood of the New Life," a community founded by Thomas Harris on the shores of Lake Erie. Harris was an American Brother Prince. He possessed all Beloved's magnetic power with all Beloved's lust for domination and all his preoccupation with the *certo balsamo.* Like Beloved, he was consistently guided to relieve his followers of all their available cash and, again like Beloved, he had invented a theology proving that he was divine and justifying him in going to bed with any woman he had a mind to. The story of Oliphant's strange servitude to the Prophet of Brocton has been

[187]

told in the biography written by his cousin, Margaret Oliphant, the novelist, I need not repeat it here, Suffice it to say that Oliphant, together with his mother, Lady Oliphant, and his wife, Alice Le Strange, remained under Harris's spell for thirteen years. Lady Oliphant, indeed, escaped only by death. Laurence and Alice broke away, after a long and scandalous conflict, in 1881. But it was only from the man Harris that they had parted, not from his ideas. Freed from his clutches, they proceeded at once to the Holy Land, where they set up a community of their own (suppressed in due course at the instance of the London Vigilance Association) and wrote in collaboration the work which I shall now describe.

The sub-title of *Sympneumata* is "Evolutionary Forces Now Active in Man." The words announce unequivocally that justification, in this case, will not be in terms of theology or religious experience, but of hard-boiled secular thought. Oliphant was addressing himself to a public that ranked *The Origin of Species* above the Apocalypse. He wanted to behave very much as Beloved and Mr. Harris had behaved; but he felt it necessary to justify this behaviour in terms of the philosophy most highly esteemed by his contemporaries. The appeal is no longer to religion but to science. True, the science is peculiar; but that does not matter. The significant fact is that Oliphant should have found it natural to use even the ridiculous parody of science for the justification of his sexual desires.

He begins his book with an account of human evolution. Originally, it appears, man was a being composed of matter in the fluid state. At a certain moment in his history there occurred "a catastrophe, of which the tradition survives in so many forms under the name of 'the fall.'" What was the nature of this catastrophe? "A precipitation of the period of reproduction"—whatever that may have been. The result was that the original, liquid man came to be encrusted with grosser matter.

A divine energy, the energy of love, radiates out from the core of every human individual. "If the action of this force could be maintained in a constant projection from the centre to the circumference, it would necessarily remain absolutely pure and holy." Unfortunately, currents flow in from the lower creation. "Rushing like a torrent towards the centre, it (the current of lower life) meets the divine outward streaming current, and produces a shock throughout the nervous system, which is utterly foreign to the orderly and divine expression of emotion."

But a change is at hand. During the nineteenth century Evolution has been producing new types of human beings, gifted with "an acute sensibility for perceiving the quality of the dynamic impulsion, that plays through the nerve fluids." This dynamic impulsion,

[189]

as we have seen, is divine; and the new, nineteenth-
century human beings discover "to their astonishment
that, while their emotions acquire a character of spir-
itualization, a delicacy and a subtle fervour, by which
they can only judge them to be discarding more and
more the earthliness of things earthly, they nevertheless
connect themselves with the physical organism by an in-
creasing sensational consciousness. . . . That disconnection between high and pathetic feeling and bodily
sensation, which has prevailed in the human mind,
ceases to be possible, and man begins to have sensational acquaintance with his interior organism, as being
the seat of his loftiest and purest emotions." That modern man should be subject to such apocalyptic sensations is not surprising; for evolution is changing his
whole structure. "Evolution's work on the superincum-
bent atoms, changing their constitution and bringing
into the spaces tenanted by the corruptible flesh atoms
developed from the inner nature of the body's form,
is bringing to these same surfaces the power to endure
the acute and intense sensations generated by divine
heat currents." "The immanence of God in man, so
much asserted and so little felt, becomes now a physical
fact; as physical as marital affection, as the ardours of
heroism, as the tremors of alarm—but more absolutely
and unmistakably physical; and acting upon the surface
with an intensity superior to that of any other known
sensation, in the degree in which it corresponds with

the more profound depth from which it has taken its rise." The new man is "a vessel charged with holy force." This force cannot act freely "unless human beings participated in the active and emotional being who is to them the sex-complement, whom we term the Sympneuma." (We recognize Harris's Counterparts and our old friends, the Affinities and Spiritual Wives.) Thanks to Evolution (blessed *deus ex machina!*), the quality of the intense vitality which God presses down upon us at this hour, burns with some fuller ardour as His sex-completeness than the world could receive before." For this reason "the value of history, of philosophy becomes nil as a basis for the deduction of theories as to what the man of this age may feel, can know, or should do."

There follows next a section of the book addressed primarily to the ladies. Evolution has changed woman as profoundly as it has changed man. The "suppression of her active powers" has been succeeded by her "surprised awakening at the embrace that steals upon her sense—as her Sympneuma's form constructs itself around and over her—presenting her at last, in those organic realms of her sub-surfaces, where she reflected before, as on a vapoury void, the confused images of dreams and disfigured truths, with a fixed organism, constructed to take up at once the waves of her deep vibrations, and through which her contact is reopened into the whole connected world of potent manhood."

[191]

But potent manhood, it obscurely appears, is not to perform its ordinary, vulgar functions. There are to be no babies, only sympneumatous sensations. "Therefore, O woman, in this age of sharp transition, there is a marvellous lesson for you to learn that has not yet been dreamt of. . . . Revive, for the airs of heaven breathe on you now to that effect, in the folded petals of your deepest nature. Body forth at last, bring forth the joy of nature's depths—man makes a new demand on you, and asks not for himself but for all people. He craves not now the commerce of the dissevered sexes, nor the production of fresh peopling in their forms, for he lives now in the expanding chambers of his own subsurfaces, where the Sympneuma's presence pervades and satisfies sensation, and bids the old activities of exterior forms make long pause, awaiting high conditions." That which has happened in the course of evolution is that which ought to have happened. Not only is it possible for modern woman to enjoy it, it is also her duty "to demand of God the draughts of the supreme elixir which waits to shower into human nature."

Not unnaturally, Oliphant regards the intellect as a danger. Its roots are too "slightly grounded in the pregnant bowels of the moral nature" to be capable of appreciating the significance of the sympneumatous revelation. Therefore get rid of the intellect; "let loose the powers of actual nature in you—man-woman, woman-man—that God may be incarnate! . . . Hurl right and left and far all claims of systems of thought and life that served of old their time, if they now cling upon your skirts and burden your free ascent. . . . Lo! on the little field of your frail nature is room for mightiest peace, for the full immensity of reconciliation to God's demands and man's—room for the meeting in you of heaven and earth." Science, in the shape of Oliphant's fluid atoms and evolving sub-surfaces, brings us to the same harbour as Patmore's Catholicism and the divine guidance of the ex-evangelical parson, Brother Prince. No, not quite to the same harbour; for through the book's dark phrases one half perceives, half guesses that Oliphant liked his *certo balsamo* in some oddly refined and alembicated form. "When he (man) has once experienced by repetition the unerring tendency of delight, intense, sensational, to visit him *spontaneously,* the painfully acquired enjoyments that he knew before, of body, intellect or spirit, fade and grow valueless." This is as near as our author ever comes to lifting the veil. One closes the book, not altogether certain of his meaning, but at any rate divining enough to know that "liberal shepherds give a grosser name" to the sympneumatous experience.

Oliphant's obscurity is lightened by the probing beam directed upon him by Mrs. Whitall Smith. A female disciple of the Oliphants told her "that Mrs. Oliphant was doing a wonderful missionary work among the Arabs in Palestine by imparting to them

what the Oliphants called 'Sympneumata,' which they
claimed was the coming of the spiritual counterpart
to the individual. She said the way Mrs. Oliphant
accomplished this was by getting into bed with these
Arabs, no matter how degraded and dirty they were,
and the contact of her body brought about, as she supposed, the coming of the counterpart. It was a great
trial for her to do this, and she felt that she was performing a most holy mission. As she was one of the
most refined and cultivated of English ladies, it is evident that nothing but a strong sense of duty could have
induced her to such a course." We have here a good
example of the way in which a philosophy invented to
justify one set of actions leads logically to the justification—nay, to the imposition as positive duties—of
other and much stranger acts, of which the justifier
originally never dreamt.

Mrs. Smith's next contact with Oliphant was through
a young lady who had been engaged to one of the
Sympneumatist's disciples. Introduced to Oliphant, she
was deeply impressed by his appearance and manner.
He gave her religious instruction, in the course of
which he "took more and more liberties with her, and
at last induced her to share his bed, with the idea that
the personal touch would bring about the sympneumata for which she so longed. . . . Finally, when he
thought the time was ripe, he began to urge her to
spread the blessing by herself enticing young men into

[194]

the same relations with her as his own." The girl was disquieted and, after taking advice, broke off her engagement. The young man remained faithful to his master. Mrs. Smith reveals the reason for this loyalty. "Mr. Oliphant's idea was that the sexual passion was the only real spiritual life, and that in order to be spiritually alive you must continually keep that passion excited. The consequence was that he could never write anything except when his passions were aroused. His influence over the young Scotchman was so great that he had induced him to believe entirely in this theory, and he too was never happy for a single moment unless his own passions were excited."

A favourite instrument of philosophical justification is the conception of *nature*. Nature, one finds, is invoked in almost every controversy about matters of conduct—not by one party only, but by both. Rebels will justify rebellion, and the orthodox their orthodoxy, in the same way—by an appeal to nature. Rebellion is in accordance with nature therefore permissible and right. Conversely, orthodoxy is right, not only because it is divinely revealed, but also because it is in accordance with nature. Thus, we learn from St. Thomas that fornication is a sin, because, among other reasons, it is unnatural. For it is "natural in the human species for the male to be able to know his own offspring for certain, because he has the education of that offspring; but the certainty would be destroyed if there were promiscuous intercourse." Therefore fornication is unnatural. If nature is that which is (and there is no other legitimate definition), then such arguments as St. Thomas's are perfectly meaningless. Some men wish to know and educate their offspring; some do not. Some indulge in fornication, some refrain. Both types of behaviour occur and we have no right to say that one is natural and the other unnatural. Writers who speak of the unnaturalness of asceticism are making the same mistake as their opponents. Asceticism, like licentiousness, is an observable fact; in other words, it is natural. For scholastically minded people, nature is not that which is; the nature of a thing is practically identical with its essence, and its essence is a metaphysical entity, not susceptible of observation. The scholastic method may be represented schematically as follows: you take a collection of beings, you set your fancy and your ingenuity to work and, out of your inner consciousness, you evolve (with the aid of such literature as you regard as authoritative) a conception of their essential character. This you call their "nature." When any member of the group in question behaves in a way which does not conform to your *a priori* conception of his essence, you say that the behaviour is unnatural. The scholastics sought to rationalize revelation by proving that revelation was in accord with nature; but what they called "nature" was entirely home-made. All they did was to justify one metaphysical conception in terms of another metaphysical conception. Owing to the vagueness and ambiguity of language, this proceeding was and still is remarkably successful. By "nature" the scholastically minded mean "metaphysical essence"; but the word also connotes "that which is." They trade on the fact that most readers attach to "nature" its second meaning and can therefore be induced to accept as a record of observation or a sober piece of inference any *a priori* absurdity which may be passed off under that reassuring name.

The thirst for rationality and righteousness is almost as insistent as the thirst for sexual pleasure and for the gratification of pride. There will always be cravings to justify and always a desire for justification. Justificatory theories are often nonsensical; but this would not greatly matter, if they justified only those desires and actions immediately responsible for their invention. The real trouble about most of these theories is that they justify and indeed logically impose upon those who accept them modes of thought and behaviour to which mere irrational cravings would never have prompted them. The cases described in the preceding pages are mainly farcical in their extravagance. It is difficult for people whose main preoccupation is sensual enjoyment to do harm on a very large scale. But where the cravings to be justified are cravings for power, glory and the like, the case is different. The tree is known by its fruits. Judged by this standard, sympneumatism, for example, is a joke; nationalism, which is a theory intrinsically almost as preposterous as poor Oliphant's, is a tragedy and a menace.

All justificatory theories are determined by the prevailing systems of philosophy and ethics. These, in their turn, are in part determined and themselves in part determine the economic and social circumstances of the age. Changes of circumstance result in changed philosophies; changed philosophies provide men with the motive power for changing circumstances. The reformer must attack simultaneously on all the fronts, from the metaphysical to the economic; if he does not, he cannot hope to achieve more than a partial success.

How can justificatory theories be made less extravagant? How can they be prevented from justifying all kinds of monstrous actions, which the original inventor of the theory never felt the impulse to perform? A complete answer to these questions would have to contain, among other things, a full-scale programme of social and economic reform and text-books—more comprehensive than any yet written—of social and individual psychology. All I can do here is to offer a few reflections on the purely intellectual aspects of the question.

All justifications in terms of science and rationalistic philosophy are ultimately utilitarian in appeal. They aim at showing that the particular action which it is desired to justify is useful, either to the individual or to the community. The science and the rationalistic argument are intended to demonstrate this utility. The cure for extravagance in these cases is knowledge. True, it is not an infallible cure. A man may know that the action he desires to perform is bad for him; but if his desire is strong enough, he will either ignore his knowledge or else manipulate it in such a way as to make it seem to justify his behaviour. The Nazi race-scientists furnish a case in point. Most of these men are highly educated; in other words, they have been given every opportunity for discovering what to the great majority of biologists outside Germany is obvious: that most of the stuff talked about Nordics and Aryans is simply rubbish. They have been given this opportunity, but they have not taken it—they have not wished to take it. Knowledge, I repeat, is not an infallible cure for extravagance in justificatory theories; but at least it sets certain obstacles in the way of extravagance. People who know the facts can never be quite so free to indulge in fantasy as those who don't.

Justification in religious terms seems to tend towards extravagance in proportion as God is thought of as personal. "Temporary suspensions of morality" are essentially personal acts; and those who are "guided" to suspend morality do so under the belief that they are receiving orders from a superior and inscrutable Divine Person. The historical records show that they persist in doing this even where theology lays it down that the Divine Person is absolutely good. Similarly, men persist

[199]

in attributing to a personal God a special interest in their own nation, even where theology has defined Him as the Father of all. That this should be so is not surprising: it is difficult, if one thinks of God as a person, not to think of Him as similar to the only persons with whom one has direct acquaintance—oneself and one's fellows.

We must ask ourselves whether belief in the personality of God is, first, logically necessary; and, second, pragmatically valuable. It is impossible in this place to set forth the arguments for and against the personality of God. The matter has been summed up by Professor Whitehead in his *Religion in the Making*, and I cannot do better than quote his words:

"There is a large concurrence in the negative doctrine that this religious experience does not include any direct intuition of a definite person, or individual. . . .

"The evidence for the assertion of general, though not universal, concurrence in the doctrine of no direct vision of a personal God, can only be found by a consideration of the religious thought of the civilized world. . . .

"Throughout India and China religious thought, so far as it has been interpreted in precise form, disclaims the intuition of any ultimate personality substantial to the universe. This is true of Confucian philosophy, Buddhist philosophy and Hindoo philosophy. There may be personal embodiments, but the substratum is impersonal.

"Christian theology has also, in the main, adopted the position that there is no direct intuition of such an ultimate personal substratum for the world. It maintains the doctrine of the existence of a personal God as a truth, but holds that our belief in it is based upon inference."

In order to calculate the pragmatic value of belief in a personal God, it would be necessary to collect and carefully weigh all the available historical and psychological evidence.

From the little I know about the subject, I should guess that the results of such an investigation would be more or less as follows. Belief in a personal God tends to heighten the believer's energy and to strengthen his will. So far so good. But energy can be used to achieve undesirable as well as desirable ends; and a strong will misdirected is the source of endless trouble. A personal God, as we have already seen, tends, in spite of all theological precautions, to be thought of as similar to a human person. Thus, it comes about that the believer feels himself justified in giving rein to such all too human tendencies as pride, anger, jealousy and hatred, by the reflection that, in doing so, he is behaving like a God who is a person. The frequency with which men have identified the prompting of their own passions with the personal guidance of God who is Himself (the sacred books affirm it) subject to passion, is really appalling. Belief in a personal God has released a vast amount of energy directed towards good ends; but it has probably released an almost equal amount of energy directed towards ends which were evil. This consideration, taken in conjunction with the philosophical improbability of the dogma, should make us extremely chary of accepting belief in a personal deity.

D. H. Lawrence

"I ALWAYS say, my motto is 'Art for my sake.' " The words are from a letter written by Lawrence before the war. "If I *want* to write, I write—and if I don't want to, I won't. The difficulty is to find exactly the form one's passion—work is produced by passion with me, like kisses—is it with you?—wants to take."

"Art for my sake." But even though for my sake, still art. Lawrence was always and unescapably an artist. Yes, unescapably is the word; for there were moments when he wanted to escape from his destiny. "I wish from the bottom of my heart that the fates had not stigmatized me 'writer.' It is a sickening business." But against the decree of fate there is no appeal. Nor was it by any means all the time that Lawrence wanted to appeal. His complaints were only occasional, and he was provoked to make them, not by any hatred of art as such, but by hatred of the pains and humiliations incidental to practising as an artist. Writing to Edward Garnett, "Why, why," he asks, "should we be plagued with literature and such-like tomfoolery? Why can't we live decent, honourable lives, without the critics in the Little Theatre fretting us?" The publication of a work of art is always the exposure of a nakedness, the throwing of something delicate and sensitive to the "asses,

[203]

apes and dogs." Mostly, however, Lawrence loved his destiny, loved the art of which he was a master—as who, that is a master, can fail to do? Besides, art, as he practised it, and as, at the bottom, every artist, even the most pharisaically "pure," practises it, was "art for my sake." It was useful to him, pragmatically helpful. "One sheds one's sicknesses in books—repeats and presents again one's emotions to be master of them." And, anyhow, liking or disliking were finally irrelevant in the face of the fact that Lawrence was in a real sense possessed by his creative genius. He could not help himself. "I am doing a novel," he writes in an early letter, "a novel which I have never grasped. Damn its eyes, there I am at p. 145 and I've no notion what it's about. I hate it. F. says it is good. But it's like a novel in a foreign language I don't know very well—I can only just make out what it's about." To this strange force within him, to this power that created his works of art, there was nothing to do but submit. Lawrence submitted, completely and with reverence. "I often think one ought to be able to pray before one works—and then leave it to the Lord. Isn't it hard work to come to real grips with one's imagination—throw everything overboard? I always feel as though I stood naked for the fire of Almighty God to go through me—and it's rather an awful feeling. One has to be so terribly religious to be an artist." Conversely, he might have added, one has to be terribly an artist, terribly conscious of "inspira-

[204]

tion" and the compelling force of genius, to be religious as Lawrence was religious.

It is impossible to write about Lawrence except as an artist. He was an artist first of all, and the fact of his being an artist explains a life which seems, if you forget it, inexplicably strange. In *Son of Woman*, Mr. Middleton Murry has written at great length about Lawrence—but about a Lawrence whom you would never suspect, from reading that curious essay in destructive hagiography, of being an artist. For Mr. Murry almost completely ignores the fact that his subject— his victim, I had almost said—was one whom "the fates had stigmatized 'writer.'" His book is *Hamlet* without the Prince of Denmark—for all its metaphysical subtleties and its Freudian ingenuities, very largely irrelevant. The absurdity of his critical method becomes the more manifest when we reflect that nobody would ever have heard of a Lawrence who was not an artist.

An artist is the sort of artist he is, because he happens to possess certain gifts. And he leads the sort of life he does in fact lead, because he is an artist, and an artist with a particular kind of mental endowment. Now there are general abilities and there are special talents. A man who is born with a great share of some special talent is probably less deeply affected by nurture than one whose ability is generalized. His gift is his fate, and he follows a predestined course, from which no ordinary power can deflect him. In spite of Helvétius and

Dr. Watson, it seems pretty obvious that no amount of education—including under that term everything from the Œdipus complex to the English Public School system—could have prevented Mozart from being a musician, or musicianship from being the central fact in Mozart's life. And how would a different education have modified the expression of, say, Blake's gift? It is, of course, impossible to answer. One can only express the unverifiable conviction that an art so profoundly individual and original, so manifestly "inspired," would have remained fundamentally the same whatever (within reasonable limits) had been the circumstances of Blake's upbringing. Lawrence, as Mr. F. R. Leavis insists, has many affinities with Blake. "He had the same gift of knowing what he was interested in, the same power of distinguishing his own feelings and emotions from conventional sentiment, the same 'terrifying honesty.' " Like Blake, like any man possessed of great special talents, he was predestined by his gifts. Explanations of him in terms of a Freudian hypothesis of nurture may be interesting, but they do not explain. That Lawrence was profoundly affected by his love for his mother and by her excessive love for him, is obvious to anyone who has read *Sons and Lovers*. None the less it is, to me at any rate, almost equally obvious that even if his mother had died when he was a child, Lawrence would still have been, essentially and fundamentally, Lawrence. Lawrence's biography does not account for

Lawrence's achievement. On the contrary, his achievement, or rather the gift that made the achievement possible, accounts for a great deal of his biography. He lived as he lived, because he was, intrinsically and from birth, what he was. If we would write intelligibly of Lawrence, we must answer, with all their implications, two questions: first, what sort of gifts did he have? and secondly, how did the possession of these gifts affect the way he responded to experience?

Lawrence's special and characteristic gift was an extraordinary sensitiveness to what Wordsworth called "unknown modes of being." He was always intensely aware of the mystery of the world, and the mystery was always for him a *numen*, divine. Lawrence could never forget, as most of us almost continuously forget, the dark presence of the otherness that lies beyond the boundaries of man's conscious mind. This special sensibility was accompanied by a prodigious power of rendering the immediately experienced otherness in terms of literary art.

Such was Lawrence's peculiar gift. His possession of it accounts for many things. It accounts, to begin with, for his attitude towards sex. His particular experiences as a son and as a lover may have intensified his preoccupation with the subject; but they certainly did not make it. Whatever his experiences, Lawrence *must* have been preoccupied with sex; his gift made it inevitable. For Lawrence, the significance of the sexual experience

[207]

was this: that, in it, the immediate, non-mental knowledge of divine otherness is brought, so to speak, to a
focus—a focus of darkness. Parodying Matthew Arnold's
famous formula, we may say that sex is something not
ourselves that makes for—not righteousness, for the essence of religion is not righteousness; there is a spiritual
world, as Kierkegaard insists, beyond the ethical—
rather, that makes for life, for divineness, for union
with the mystery. Paradoxically, this something not ourselves is yet a something lodged within us; this quintessence of otherness is yet the quintessence of our proper
being. "And God the Father, the Inscrutable, the Un-
knowable, we know in the flesh, in Woman. She is the
door for our in-going and our out-coming. In her we go
back to the Father; but like the witnesses of the trans-
figuration, blind and unconscious." Yes, blind and unconscious; otherwise it is a revelation, not of divine
otherness, but of very human evil. "The embrace of
love, which should bring darkness and oblivion, would
with these lovers (the hero and heroine of one of Poe's
tales) be a daytime thing, bringing more heightened
consciousness, visions, spectrum-visions, prismatic. The
evil thing that daytime love-making is, and all sex-
palaver!" How Lawrence hated Eleonora and Ligeia
and Roderick Usher and all such soulful Mrs. Shandies,
male as well as female! What a horror, too, he had of
all Don Juans, all knowing sensualists and conscious
libertines! (About the time he was writing *Lady Chat-*

terley's Lover he read the memoirs of Casanova, and was profoundly shocked.) And how bitterly he loathed the Wilhelm-Meisterish view of love as an education, as a means to culture, a Sandow-exerciser for the soul! To *use* love in this way, consciously and deliberately, seemed to Lawrence wrong, almost a blasphemy. "It seems to me queer," he says to a fellow-writer, "that you prefer to present men chiefly—as if you cared for women not so much for what they were in themselves as for what the men saw in them. So that after all in your work women seem not to have an existence, save they are the projections of the men. . . . It's the *positivity* of women you seem to deny—make them sort of instrumental." The instrumentality of Wilhelm Meister's women shocked Lawrence profoundly.

(Here, in a parenthesis, let me remark on the fact that Lawrence's doctrine is constantly invoked by people, of whom Lawrence himself would passionately have disapproved, in defence of a behaviour which he would have found deplorable or even revolting. That this should have happened is by no means, of course, a condemnation of the doctrine. The same philosophy of life may be good or bad according as the person who accepts it and lives by it is intrinsically fine or base. Tartufe's doctrine was the same, after all, as Pascal's. There have been refined fetish-worshippers, and unspeakably swinish Christians. To the preacher of a new way of life the most depressing thing that can happen

is, surely, success. For success permits him to see how
those he has converted distort and debase and make
ignoble parodies of his teaching. If Francis of Assisi had
lived to be a hundred, what bitterness he would have
tasted! Happily for the saint, he died at forty-five, still
relatively undisillusioned, because still on the threshold
of the great success of his order. Writers influence their
readers, preachers their auditors—but always, at bottom, to be more themselves. If the reader's self happens
to be intrinsically similar to the writer's, then the influence is what the writer would wish it to be. If he is
intrinsically unlike the writer, then he will probably
twist the writer's doctrine into a rationalization of beliefs, an excuse for behaviour, wholly alien to the beliefs
and behaviour approved by the writer. Lawrence has
suffered the fate of every man whose works have exercised an influence upon his fellows. It was inevitable
and in the nature of things.)

For someone with a gift for sensing the mystery of
otherness, true love must necessarily be, in Lawrence's
vocabulary, *nocturnal*. So must true knowledge. Nocturnal and tactual—a touching in the night. Man in-
habits, for his own convenience, a home-made universe
within the greater alien world of external matter and
his own irrationality. Out of the illimitable blackness
of that world the light of his customary thinking scoops,
as it were, a little illuminated cave—a tunnel of bright-
ness, in which, from the birth of consciousness to its

death, he lives, moves and has his being. For most of us this bright tunnel is the whole world. We ignore the outer darkness; or if we cannot ignore it, if it presses too insistently upon us, we disapprove, being afraid. Not so Lawrence. He had eyes that could see, beyond the walls of light, far into the darkness, sensitive fingers that kept him continually aware of the environing mystery. He could not be content with the home-made, human tunnel, could not conceive that anyone else should be content with it. Moreover—and in this he was unlike those others, to whom the world's mystery is continuously present, the great philosophers and men of science—he did not want to increase the illuminated area; he approved of the outer darkness, he felt at home in it. Most men live in a little puddle of light thrown by the gig-lamps of habit and their immediate interest; but there is also the pure and powerful illumination of the disinterested scientific intellect. To Lawrence, both lights were suspect, both seemed to falsify what was, for him, the immediately apprehended reality—the darkness of mystery. "My great religion," he was already saying in 1912, "is a belief in the blood, the flesh, as being wiser than the intellect. We can go wrong in our minds. But what the blood feels, and believes, and says, is always true." Like Blake, who had prayed to be delivered from "single vision and Newton's sleep": like Keats, who had drunk destruction to Newton for having explained the rainbow, Lawrence disapproved of too much knowledge, on the score that it diminished men's sense of wonder and blunted their sensitiveness to the great mystery. His dislike of science was passionate and expressed itself in the most fantastically unreasonable terms. "All scientists are liars," he would say, when I brought up some experimentally established fact, which he happened to dislike. "Liars, liars!" It was a most convenient theory. I remember in particular one long and violent argument on evolution, in the reality of which Lawrence always passionately disbelieved. "But look at the evidence, Lawrence," I insisted, "look at all the evidence." His answer was characteristic. "But I don't care about evidence. Evidence doesn't mean anything to me. I don't feel it *here*." And he pressed his two hands on his solar plexus. I abandoned the argument and thereafter never, if I could avoid it, mentioned the hated name of science in his presence. Lawrence could give so much, and what he gave was so valuable, that it was absurd and profitless to spend one's time with him disputing about a matter in which he absolutely refused to take a rational interest. Whatever the intellectual consequences, he remained through thick and thin unshakably loyal to his own genius. The *daimon* which possessed him was, he felt, a divine thing, which he would never deny or explain away, never even ask to accept a compromise. This loyalty to his own self, or rather to his gift, to the strange and powerful *numen* which, he felt, used him as its taber-

nacle, is fundamental in Lawrence and accounts, as
nothing else can do, for all that the world found strange
in his beliefs and his behaviour. It was not an incapacity to understand that made him reject those generalizations and abstractions by means of which the
philosophers and the men of science try to open a path
for the human spirit through the chaos of phenomena.
Not incapacity, I repeat; for Lawrence had, over and
above his peculiar gift, an extremely acute intelligence.
He was a clever man as well as a man of genius. (In his
boyhood and adolescence he had been a great passer
of examinations.) He could have understood the aim
and methods of science perfectly well if he had wanted
to. Indeed, he did understand them perfectly well;
and it was for that very reason that he rejected them.
For the methods of science and critical philosophy were
incompatible with the exercise of his gift—the immediate perception and artistic rendering of divine otherness. And their aim, which is to push back the frontier
of the unknown, was not to be reconciled with his aim,
which was to remain as intimately as possible in contact with the surrounding darkness. And so, in spite of
their enormous prestige, he rejected science and critical
philosophy; he remained loyal to his gift. Exclusively
loyal. He would not attempt to qualify or explain his
immediate knowledge of the mystery, would not even
attempt to supplement it by other, abstract knowledge.
"These terrible, conscious birds, like Poe and his

Ligeia deny the very life that is in them; they want to turn it all into talk, into *knowing*. And so life, which will not be known, leaves them." Lawrence refused to *know* abstractly. He preferred to live; and he wanted other people to live.

No man is by nature complete and universal; he cannot have first-hand knowledge of every kind of possible human experience. Universality, therefore, can only be achieved by those who mentally simulate living experience—by the knowers, in a word, by people like Goethe (an artist for whom Lawrence always felt the most intense repugnance).

Again, no man is by nature perfect, and none can spontaneously achieve perfection. The greatest gift is a limited gift. Perfection, whether ethical or aesthetic, must be the result of knowing and of the laborious application of knowledge. Formal aesthetics are an affair of rules and the best classical models; formal morality, of the ten commandments and the imitation of Christ.

Lawrence would have nothing to do with proceedings so "unnatural," so disloyal to the gift, to the resident or visiting *numen*. Hence his aesthetic principle, that art must be wholly spontaneous, and, like the artist, imperfect, limited and transient. Hence, too, his ethical principle, that a man's first moral duty is not to attempt to live above his human station, or beyond his inherited psychological income.

The great work of art and the monument more per-

ennial than brass are, in their very perfection and ever-
lastingness, inhuman—too much of a good thing.
Lawrence did not approve of them. Art, he thought,
should flower from an immediate impulse towards self-
expression or communication, and should wither with
the passing of the impulse. Of all building materials
Lawrence liked adobe the best; its extreme plasticity
and extreme impermanence endeared it to him. There
could be no everlasting pyramids in adobe, no mathematically accurate Parthenons. Nor, thank heaven, in
wood. Lawrence loved the Etruscans, among other
reasons, because they built wooden temples, which have
not survived. Stone oppressed him with its indestruct-
ible solidity, its capacity to take and indefinitely keep
the hard uncompromising forms of pure geometry.
Great buildings made him feel uncomfortable, even
when they were beautiful. He felt something of the
same discomfort in the presence of any highly finished
work of art. In music, for example, he liked the folk-
song, because it was a slight thing, born of immediate
impulse. The symphony oppressed him; it was too big,
too elaborate, too carefully and consciously worked out,
too "would-be"—to use a characteristic Lawrencian
expression. He was quite determined that none of his
writings should be "would-be." He allowed them to
flower as they liked from the depths of his being and
would never use his conscious intellect to force them
into a semblance of more than human perfection, or

more than human universality. It was characteristic of him that he hardly ever corrected or patched what he had written. I have often heard him say, indeed, that he was incapable of correcting. If he was dissatisfied with what he had written, he did not, as most authors do, file, clip, insert, transpose; he rewrote. In other words, he gave the *daimon* another chance to say what it wanted to say. There are, I believe, three complete and totally distinct manuscripts of *Lady Chatterley's Lover*. Nor was this by any means the only novel that he wrote more than once. He was determined that all he produced should spring direct from the mysterious, irrational source of power within him. The conscious intellect should never be allowed to come and impose, after the event, its abstract pattern of perfection.

It was the same in the sphere of ethics as in that of art. "They want me to have form: that means, they want me to have *their* pernicious, ossiferous, skin-and-grief form, and I won't." This was written about his novels; but it is just as applicable to his life. Every man, Lawrence insisted, must be an artist in life, must create his own moral form. The art of living is harder than the art of writing. "It is a much more delicate thing to make love, and win love, than to declare love." All the more reason, therefore, for practising this art with the most refined and subtle sensibility; all the more reason for not accepting that "pernicious skin-and-grief form" of morality, which *they* are always try-

ing to impose on one. It is the business of the sensitive
artist in life to accept his own nature as it is, not to try
to force it into another shape. He must take the material given him—the weaknesses and irrationalities,
as well as the sense and the virtues; the mysterious
darkness and otherness no less than the light of reason
and the conscious ego—must take them all and weave
them together into a satisfactory pattern; *his* pattern,
not somebody else's pattern. "Once I said to myself:
'How can I blame—why be angry?' . . . Now I say:
'When anger comes with bright eyes, he may do his
will. In me he will hardly shake off the hand of God.
He is one of the archangels, with a fiery sword. God
sent him—it is beyond my knowing.' " This was written in 1910. Even at the very beginning of his career
Lawrence was envisaging man as simply the locus of
a polytheism. Given his particular gifts of sensitiveness
and of expression it was inevitable. Just as it was inevitable that a man of Blake's peculiar genius should
formulate the very similar doctrine of the independence
of states of being. All the generally accepted systems of
philosophy and of ethics aim at policing man's polytheism in the name of some Jehovah of intellectual and
moral consistency. For Lawrence this was an indefen-
sible proceeding. One god had as much right to exist
as another, and the dark ones were as genuinely divine
as the bright. Perhaps (since Lawrence was so specially
sensitive to the quality of dark godhead and so specially

gifted to express it in art), perhaps even more divine. Anyhow, the polytheism was a democracy. This conception of human nature resulted in the formulation of two rather surprising doctrines, one ontological and the other ethical. The first is what I may call the Doctrine of Cosmic Pointlessness. "There is no point. Life and Love are life and love, a bunch of violets is a bunch of violets, and to drag in the idea of a point is to ruin everything. Live and let live, love and let love, flower and fade, and follow the natural curve, which flows on, pointless."

Ontological pointlessness has its ethical counterpart in the doctrine of insouciance. "They simply are eaten up with caring. They are so busy caring about Fascism or Leagues of Nations or whether France is right or whether Marriage is threatened, that they never know where they are. They certainly never live on the spot where they are. They inhabit abstract space, the desert void of politics, principles, right and wrong, and so forth. They are doomed to be abstract. Talking to them is like trying to have a human relationship with the letter x in algebra." As early as 1911 his advice to his sister was: "Don't meddle with religion. I would leave all that alone, if I were you, and try to occupy myself fully in the present."

Reading such passages—and they abound in every book that Lawrence wrote—I am always reminded of that section of the *Pensées* in which Pascal speaks of the absurd distractions with which men fill their leisure, so that there shall be no hole or cranny left for a serious thought to lodge itself in their consciousness. Lawrence also inveighs against *divertissements*, but not against the same *divertissements* as Pascal. For him, there were two great and criminal distractions. First, work, which he regarded as a mere stupefacient, like opium. ("Don't exhaust yourself too much," he writes to an industrious friend; "it is immoral." Immoral, because, among other reasons, it is too easy, a shirking of man's first duty, which is to live. "Think of the rest and peace, the positive sloth and luxury of idleness that work is." Lawrence had a real puritan's disapproval of the vice of working. He attacked the gospel of work for the same reasons as Chrysippus attacked Aristotle's gospel of pure intellectualism—on the ground that it was, in the old Stoic's words, "only a kind of amusement" and that real living was a more serious affair than labour or abstract speculations.) The other inexcusable distraction, in Lawrence's eyes, was "spirituality," that lofty musing on the ultimate nature of things which constitutes, for Pascal, "the whole dignity and business of man." Pascal was horrified that human beings could so far forget the infinite and the eternal as to "dance and play the lute and sing and make verses." Lawrence was no less appalled that they could so far forget all the delights and difficulties of immediate living as to remember eternity and infinity, to say nothing of the League of

[219]

Nations and the Sanctity of Marriage. Both were great artists and so each is able to convince us that he is at any rate partly right. Just how far each is right, this is not the place to discuss. Nor, indeed, is the question susceptible of a definite answer. "Mental consciousness," wrote Lawrence, "is a purely individual affair. Some men are born to be highly and delicately conscious." Some are not. Moreover, each of the ages of man has its suitable philosophy of life. (Lawrence's, I should say, was not a very good philosophy for old age or failing powers.) Besides, there are certain conjunctions of circumstances in which spontaneous living is the great distraction and certain others in which it is almost criminal to divert oneself with eternity or the League of Nations. Lawrence's peculiar genius was such that he insisted on spontaneous living to the exclusion of ideals and fixed principles; on intuition to the exclusion of abstract reasoning. Pascal, with a very different gift, evolved, inevitably, a very different philosophy.

Lawrence's dislike of abstract knowledge and pure spirituality made him a kind of mystical materialist. Thus, the moon affects him strongly; therefore it cannot be a "stony cold world, like a world of our own gone cold. Nonsense. It is a globe of dynamic substance, like radium or phosphorus, coagulated upon a vivid pole of energy." Matter must be intrinsically as lively as the mind which perceives it and is moved by the perception. Vivid and violent spiritual effects must have correspondingly vivid and violent material causes. And, conversely, any violent feeling or desire in the mind must be capable of producing violent effects upon external matter. Lawrence could not bring himself to believe that the spirit can be moved, moved even to madness, without imparting the smallest corresponding movement to the external world. He was a subjectivist as well as a materialist; in other words, he believed in the possibility, in some form or another, of magic. Lawrence's mystical materialism found characteristic expression in the curious cosmology and physiology of his speculative essays, and in his restatement of the strange Christian doctrine of the resurrection of the body. To his mind, the survival of the spirit was not enough; for the spirit is a man's conscious identity, and Lawrence did not want to be always identical to himself; he wanted to know otherness—to know it by being it, know it in the living flesh, which is always essentially *other*. Therefore there must be a resurrection of the body.

Loyalty to his genius left him no choice; Lawrence had to insist on those mysterious forces of otherness which are scattered without, and darkly concentrated within, the body and mind of man. He had to, even though, by doing so, he imposed upon himself as a writer of novels, a very serious handicap. For according to his view of things most of men's activities were

more or less criminal distractions from the proper business of human living. He refused to write of such distractions; that is to say, he refused to write of the main
activities of the contemporary world. But as though
this drastic limitation of his subject were not sufficient, he went still further and, in some of his novels,
refused even to write of human personalities in the
accepted sense of the term. *The Rainbow and Women
in Love* (and indeed to a lesser extent all his novels)
are the practical applications of a theory, which is set
forth in a very interesting and important letter to Edward Garnett, dated June 5th, 1914. "Somehow, that
which is physic—non-human in humanity, is more interesting to me than the old-fashioned human element,
which causes one to conceive a character in a certain
moral scheme and make him consistent. The certain
moral scheme is what I object to. In Turgenev, and in
Tolstoi, and in Dostoievsky, the moral scheme into
which all the characters fit—and it is nearly the same
scheme—is, whatever the extraordinariness of the characters themselves, dull, old, dead. When Marinetti
writes: 'It is the solidity of a blade of steel that is interesting by itself, that is, the incomprehending and
inhuman alliance of its molecules in resistance to, let
us say, a bullet. The heat of a piece of wood or iron
is in fact more passionate, for us, than the laughter or
tears of a woman'—then I know what he means. He is
stupid, as an artist, for contrasting the heat of the iron

[222]

and the laugh of the woman. Because what is interesting in the laugh of the woman is the same as the binding of the molecules of steel or their action in heat: it is the inhuman will, call it physiology, or like Marinetti, physiology of matter, that fascinates me. I don't so much care about what the woman *feels*—in the ordinary usage of the word. That presumes an *ego* to feel with. I only care about what the woman *is*—what she is —inhumanly, physiologically, materially—according to the use of the word. . . . You mustn't look in my novel for the old stable *ego* of the character. There is another *ego*, according to whose action the individual is unrecognizable, and passes through, as it were, allotropic states which it needs a deeper sense than any we've been used to exercise, to discover are states of the same single radically unchanged element. (Like as diamond and coal are the same pure single element of carbon. The ordinary novel would trace the history of the diamond —but I say, 'Diamond, what! This is carbon.' And my diamond might be coal or soot, and my theme is carbon.) "

The dangers and difficulties of this method are obvious. Criticizing Stendhal, Professor Saintsbury long since remarked on "that psychological realism which is perhaps a more different thing from psychological reality than our clever ones for two generations have been willing to admit, or, perhaps, able to perceive."

Psychological reality, like physical reality, is determined by our mental and bodily make-up. Common sense, working on the evidence supplied by our unaided senses, postulates a world in which physical reality consists of such things as solid tables and chairs, bits of coal, water, air. Carrying its investigations further, science discovers that these samples of physical reality are "really" composed of atoms of different elements, and these atoms, in their turn, are "really" composed of more or less numerous electrons and protons arranged in a variety of patterns. Similarly, there is a common-sense, pragmatic conception of psychological reality and also an un-common-sense conception. For ordinary practical purposes we conceive human beings as creatures with characters. But analysis of their behaviour can be carried so far, that they cease to have characters and reveal themselves as collections of psychological atoms. Lawrence (as might have been expected of a man who could always perceive the otherness behind the most reassuringly familiar phenomenon) took the un-common-sense view of psychology. Hence the strangeness of his novels and hence also, it must be admitted, certain qualities of violent monotony and intense indistinctness, qualities which make some of them, for all their richness and their unexpected beauty, so curiously difficult to get through. Most of us are more interested in diamonds and coal than in undifferentiated carbon, however vividly described. I have known readers whose reaction to Lawrence's

[224]

books was very much the same as Lawrence's own reaction to the theory of evolution. What he wrote meant nothing to them because they "did not feel it *here*"— in the solar plexus. (That Lawrence, the hater of scientific knowing, should have applied to psychology methods which he himself compared to those of chemical analysis, may seem strange. But we must remember that his analysis was done, not intellectually, but by an immediate process of intuition; that he was able, as it were, to *feel* the carbon in diamonds and coal, to *taste* the hydrogen and oxygen in his glass of water.)

Lawrence, then, possessed, or, if you care to put it the other way round, was possessed by, a gift—a gift to which he was unshakably loyal. I have tried to show how the possession and the loyalty influenced his thinking and writing. How did they affect his life? The answer shall be, as far as possible, in Lawrence's own words. To Catherine Carswell Lawrence once wrote: "I think you are the only woman I have met who is so intrinsically detached, so essentially separate and isolated, as to be a real writer or artist or recorder. Your relations with other people are only excursions from yourself. And to want children, and common human fulfilments, is rather a falsity for you, I think. You were never made to 'meet and mingle,' but to remain intact, *essentially*, whatever your experiences may be."

Lawrence's knowledge of "the artist" was manifestly personal knowledge. He knew by actual experience that the "real writer" is an essentially separate being, who must not desire to meet and mingle and who betrays himself when he hankers too yearningly after common human fulfilments. All artists know these facts about their species, and many of them have recorded their knowledge. Recorded it, very often, with distress; being intrinsically detached is no joke. Lawrence certainly suffered his whole life from the essential solitude to which his gift condemned him. "What ails me," he wrote to the psychologist, Dr. Trigant Burrow, "is the absolute frustration of my primeval societal instinct. . . . I think societal instinct much deeper than sex instinct—and societal repression much more devastating. There is no repression of the sexual individual comparable to the repression of the societal man in me, by the individual ego, my own and everybody else's. . . . Myself, I suffer badly from being so cut off. . . . At times one is *forced* to be essentially a hermit. I don't want to be. But anything else is either a personal tussle, or a money tussle; sickening: except, of course, just for ordinary acquaintance, which remains acquaintance. One has no real human relations—that is so devastating." One has no real human relations: it is the complaint of every artist. The artist's first duty is to his genius, his *daimon*; he cannot serve two masters. Lawrence, as it happened, had an extraordinary gift for establishing an intimate relationship with almost anyone he met. "Here" (in the Bournemouth boarding-house where he

[226]

was staying after his illness, in 1912), "I get mixed up in people's lives so—it's very interesting, sometimes a bit painful, often jolly. But I run to such close intimacy with folk, it is complicating. But I love to have myself in a bit of a tangle." His love for his art was greater, however, than his love for a tangle; and whenever the tangle threatened to compromise his activities as an artist, it was the tangle that was sacrificed: he retired. Lawrence's only deep and abiding human relationship was with his wife. ("It is hopeless for me," he wrote to a fellow-artist, "to try to do anything without I have a woman at the back of me. . . . Böcklin—or somebody like him—daren't sit in a café except with his back to the wall. I daren't sit in the world without a woman behind me. . . . A woman that I love sort of keeps me in direct communication with the unknown, in which otherwise I am a bit lost.") For the rest, he was condemned by his gift to an essential separateness. Often, it is true, he blamed the world for his exile. "And it comes to this, that the *oneness* of mankind is destroyed in me (by the war). I am I, and you are you, and all heaven and hell lie in the chasm between. Believe me, I am infinitely hurt by being thus torn off from the body of mankind, but so it is and it is right." It was right because, in reality, it was not the war that had torn him from the body of mankind; it was his own talent, the strange divinity to which he owed his primary allegiance. "I will not live any more

in this time," he wrote on another occasion. "I know
what it is. I reject it. As far as I possibly can, I will
stand outside this time. I will live my life and, if possible, be happy. Though the whole world slides in
horror down into the bottomless pit . . . I believe that
the highest virtue is to be happy, living in the greatest
truth, not submitting to the falsehood of these personal
times." The adjective is profoundly significant. Of all
the possible words of disparagement which might be
applied to our uneasy age "personal" is surely about the
last that would occur to most of us. To Lawrence it
was the first. His gift was a gift of feeling and rendering the unknown, the mysteriously other. To one possessed by such a gift, almost any age would have seemed
unduly and dangerously personal. He had to reject and
escape. But when he had escaped, he could not help
deploring the absence of "real human relationships."
Spasmodically, he tried to establish contact with the
body of mankind. There were the recurrent projects for
colonies in remote corners of the earth; they all fell
through. There were his efforts to join existing political
organizations; but somehow "I seem to have lost touch
altogether with the 'Progressive' clique. In Croydon,
the Socialists are so stupid and the Fabians so flat."
(Not only in Croydon, alas.) Then, during the war,
there was his plan to cooperate with a few friends to
take independent political action; but "I would like
to be remote, in Italy, writing my soul's words. To have

to speak in the body is a violation to me." And in the end he wouldn't violate himself; he remained aloof, remote, "essentially separate." "It isn't scenery one lives by," he wrote from Cornwall in 1916, "but the freedom of moving about alone." How acutely he suffered from this freedom by which he lived! *Kangaroo* describes a later stage of the debate between the solitary artist and the man who wanted social responsibilities and contact with the body of mankind. Lawrence, like the hero of his novel, decided against contact. He was by nature not a leader of men, but a prophet, a voice crying in the wilderness—the wilderness of his own isolation. The desert was his place, and yet he felt himself an exile in it. To Rolf Gardiner he wrote, in 1926: "I should love to be connected with something, with some few people, in something. As far as anything *matters,* I have always been very much alone, and regretted it. But I can't belong to clubs, or societies, or Freemasons, or any other damn thing. So if there is, with you, an activity I *can* belong to, I shall thank my stars. But, of course, I shall be wary beyond words, of committing myself." He was in fact so wary that he never committed himself, but died remote and unconnected as he had lived. The *daimon* would not allow it to be otherwise.

(Whether Lawrence might not have been happier if he had disobeyed his *daimon* and forced himself at least into mechanical and external connection with the

body of mankind, I forbear to speculate. Spontaneity
is not the only and infallible secret of happiness; nor
is a "would-be" existence necessarily disastrous. But this
is by the way.)

It was, I think, the sense of being cut off that sent
Lawrence on his restless wanderings round the earth.
His travels were at once a flight and a search: a search
for some society with which he could establish contact,
for a world where the times were not personal and conscious knowing had not yet perverted living; a search
and at the same time a flight from the miseries and evils
of the society into which he had been born, and for
which, in spite of his artist's detachment, he could not
help feeling profoundly responsible. He felt himself
"English in the teeth of all the world, even in the teeth
of England": that was why he had to go to Ceylon and
Australia and Mexico. He could not have felt so intensely English in England without involving himself
in corporative political action, without belonging and
being attached; but to attach himself was something
he could not bring himself to do, something that the
artist in him felt as a violation. He was at once too
English and too intensely an artist to stay at home. "Perhaps it is necessary for me to try these places, perhaps
it is my destiny to know the world. It only excites the
outside of me. The inside it leaves more isolated and
stoic than ever. That's how it is. It is all a form of
running away from oneself and the great problems, all

[230]

this wild west and the strange Australia. But I try to keep quite clear. One forms not the faintest inward attachment, especially here in America."

His search was as fruitless as his flight was ineffective. He could not escape either from his homesickness or his sense of responsibility; and he never found a society to which he could belong. In a kind of despair, he plunged yet deeper into the surrounding mystery, into the dark night of that otherness whose essence and symbol is the sexual experience. In *Lady Chatterley's Lover* Lawrence wrote the epilogue to his travels and, from his long and fruitless experience of flight and search, drew what was, for him, the inevitable moral. It is a strange and beautiful book; but inexpressibly sad. But then so, at bottom, was its author's life.

Lawrence's psychological isolation resulted, as we have seen, in his seeking physical isolation from the body of mankind. This physical isolation reacted upon his thoughts. "Don't mind if I am impertinent," he wrote to one of his correspondents at the end of a rather dogmatic letter. "Living here alone one gets so different—sort of ex-cathedra." To live in isolation, above the medley, has its advantages; but it also imposes certain penalties. Those who take a bird's eye view of the world often see clearly and comprehensively; but they tend to ignore all tiresome details, all the difficulties of social life and, ignoring, to judge too sweepingly and to condemn too lightly. Nietzsche spent his most fruitful years perched on the tops of mountains, or plunged in the yet more abysmal solitude of boarding houses by the Mediterranean. That was why, a delicate and sensitive man, he could be so bloodthirstily censorious— so wrong, for all his gifts, as well as so right. From the deserts of New Mexico, from rustic Tuscany or Sicily, from the Australian bush, Lawrence observed and judged and advised the distant world of men. The judgments, as might be expected, were often sweeping and violent; the advice, though admirable as far as it went, inadequate. Political advice from even the most greatly gifted of religious innovators is always inadequate; for it is never, at bottom, advice about politics, but always about something else. Differences in quantity, if sufficiently great, produce differences of quality. This sheet of paper, for example, is qualitatively different from the electrons of which it is composed. An analogous difference divides the politician's world from the world of the artist, or the moralist, or the religious teacher. "It is the business of the artist," writes Lawrence, "to follow it (the war) to the heart of the individual fighters—not to talk in armies and nations and numbers—but to track it home—home—their war— and it's at the bottom of almost every Englishman's heart—the war—the desire of war—the *will* to war— and at the bottom of every German heart." But an appeal to the individual heart can have very little effect on politics, which is a science of averages. An actuary can tell you how many people are likely to commit suicide next year; and no artist or moralist or Messiah can, by an appeal to the individual heart, prevent his forecast from being remarkably correct. If the things which are Caesar's differ from the things which are God's, it is because Caesar's things are numbered by the thousands and millions, whereas God's things are single individual souls. The things of Lawrence's Dark God were not even individual souls; they were the psychological atoms whose patterned coming together constitutes a soul. When Lawrence offers political advice, it refers to matters which are not really political at all. The political world of enormous numbers was to him a nightmare, and he fled from it. Primitive communities are so small that their politics are essentially unpolitical; that, for Lawrence, was one of their greatest charms. Looking back from some far-away and underpopulated vantage-point at the enormous, innumerable modern world, he was appalled by what he saw. He condemned, he advised, but at bottom and finally he felt himself impotent to deal with Caesar's alien and inhuman problems. "I wish there were miracles," was his final despairing comment. "I am tired of the old laborious way of working things to their conclusions." But, alas, there are no miracles, and faith, even the faith of a man of genius, moves no mountains.

Enough of explanation and interpretation. To those who knew Lawrence, not *why*, but *that* he was what he happened to be, is the important fact. I remember very clearly my first meeting with him. The place was London, the time 1915. But Lawrence's passionate talk was of the geographically remote and of the personally very near. Of the horrors in the middle distance—war, winter, the town—he would not speak. For he was on the point, so he imagined, of setting off to Florida—to Florida, where he was going to plant that colony of escape, of which up to the last he never ceased to dream. Sometimes the name and site of this seed of a happier and different world were purely fanciful. It was called Rananim, for example, and was an island like Prospero's. Sometimes it had its place on the map and its name was Florida, Cornwall, Sicily, Mexico and again, for a time, the English countryside. That wintry afternoon in 1915 it was Florida. Before tea was over he asked me if I would join the colony, and though I was an intellectually cautious young man, not at all inclined to enthusiasms, though Lawrence had startled and embarrassed me with sincerities of a kind to which my upbringing had not accustomed me, I answered yes.

Fortunately, no doubt, the Florida scheme fell through. Cities of God have always crumbled, and Lawrence's city—his village, rather, for he hated cities —his Village of the Dark God would doubtless have disintegrated like all the rest. It was better that it should have remained, as it was always to remain, a project and a hope. And I knew this even as I said

I would join the colony. But there was something about Lawrence which made such knowledge, when one was in his presence, curiously irrelevant. He might propose impracticable schemes, he might say or write things that were demonstrably incorrect or even, on occasion (as when he talked about science), absurd. But to a very considerable extent it didn't matter. What mattered was always Lawrence himself, was the fire that burned within him, that glowed with so strange and marvellous a radiance in almost all he wrote.

My second meeting with Lawrence took place some years later, during one of his brief revisitings of that after-war England, which he had come so much to dread and to dislike. Then in 1925, while in India, I received a letter from Spotorno. He had read some essays I had written on Italian travel; said he liked them; suggested a meeting. The next year we were in Florence and so was he. From that time, till his death, we were often together—at Florence, at Forte dei Marmi, for a whole winter at Diablerets, at Bandol, in Paris, at Chexbres, at Forte again, and finally at Vence where he died.

In a spasmodically kept diary I find this entry under the date of December 27th, 1927: "Lunched and spent the p.m. with the Lawrences. D.H.L. in admirable form, talking wonderfully. He is one of the few people I feel real respect and admiration for. Of most other eminent people I have met I feel that at any rate I be-

long to the same species as they do. But this man has
something different and superior in kind, not degree."

"Different and superior in kind." I think almost
everyone who knew him well must have felt that Lawrence was this. A being, somehow, of another order,
more sensitive, more highly conscious, more capable of
feeling than even the most gifted of common men. He
had, of course, his weaknesses and defects; he had his
intellectual limitations—limitations which he seemed
to have deliberately imposed upon himself. But these
weaknesses and defects and limitations did not affect
the fact of his superior otherness. They diminished him
quantitatively, so to speak; whereas the otherness was
qualitative. Spill half your glass of wine and what remains is still wine. Water, however full the glass may
be, is always tasteless and without colour.

To be with Lawrence was a kind of adventure, a
voyage of discovery into newness and otherness. For,
being himself of a different order, he inhabited a different universe from that of common men—a brighter
and intenser world, of which, while he spoke, he would
make you free. He looked at things with the eyes, so it
seemed, of a man who had been at the brink of death
and to whom, as he emerges from the darkness, the
world reveals itself as unfathomably beautiful and
mysterious. For Lawrence, existence was one continuous convalescence; it was as though he were newly
reborn from a mortal illness every day of his life. What

[236]

these convalescent eyes saw, his most casual speech would reveal. A walk with him in the country was a walk through that marvellously rich and significant landscape which is at once the background and the principal personage of all his novels. He seemed to know, by personal experience, what it was like to be a tree or a daisy or a breaking wave or even the mysterious moon itself. He could get inside the skin of an animal and tell you in the most convincing detail how it felt and how, dimly, inhumanly, it thought. Of Black-Eyed Susan, for example, the cow at his New Mexican ranch, he was never tired of speaking, nor was I ever tired of listening to his account of her character and her bovine philosophy.

"He sees," Vernon Lee once said to me, "more than a human being ought to see. Perhaps," she added, "that's why he hates humanity so much." Why also he loved it so much. And not only humanity: nature too, and even the supernatural. For wherever he looked, he saw more than a human being ought to see; saw more and therefore loved and hated more. To be with him was to find oneself transported to one of the frontiers of human consciousness. For an inhabitant of the safe metropolis of thought and feeling it was a most exciting experience.

One of the great charms of Lawrence as a companion was that he could never be bored and so could never be boring. He was able to absorb himself completely in what he was doing at the moment; and he regarded no task as too humble for him to undertake, nor so trivial that it was not worth his while to do it well. He could cook, he could sew, he could darn a stocking and milk a cow, he was an efficient wood-cutter and a good hand at embroidery, fires always burned when he had laid them, and a floor, after Lawrence had scrubbed it, was thoroughly clean. Moreover, he possessed what is, for a highly strung and highly intelligent man, an even more remarkable accomplishment: he knew how to do nothing. He could just sit and be perfectly content. And his contentment, while one remained in his company, was infectious.

As infectious as Lawrence's contented placidity were his high spirits and his laughter. Even in the last years of his life, when his illness had got the upper hand and was killing him inch-meal, Lawrence could still laugh, on occasion, with something of the old and exuberant gaiety. Often, alas, towards the end, the laughter was bitter, and the high spirits almost terrifyingly savage. I have heard him sometimes speak of men and their ways with a kind of demoniac mockery, to which it was painful, for all the extraordinary brilliance and profundity of what he said, to listen. The secret consciousness of his dissolution filled the last years of his life with an overpowering sadness. (How tragically the splendid curve of the letters droops, at the end, towards the darkness!) It was, however, in terms of anger that he chose to express this sadness. Emotional indecency always shocked him profoundly, and, since anger seemed to him less indecent as an emotion than a resigned or complaining melancholy, he preferred to be angry. He took his revenge on the fate that had made him sad by fiercely deriding everything. And because the sadness of the slowly dying man was so unspeakably deep, his mockery was frighteningly savage. The laughter of the earlier Lawrence and, on occasion, as I have said, even the later Lawrence was without bitterness and wholly delightful.

Vitality has the attractiveness of beauty, and in Lawrence there was a continuously springing fountain of vitality. It went on welling up in him, leaping, now and then, into a great explosion of bright foam and iridescence, long after the time when, by all the rules of medicine, he should have been dead. For the last two years he was like a flame burning on in miraculous disregard of the fact that there was no more fuel to justify its existence. One grew, in spite of constantly renewed alarms, so well accustomed to seeing the flame blazing away, self-fed, in its broken and empty lamp that one almost came to believe that the miracle would be prolonged indefinitely. But it could not be. When, after several months of separation, I saw him again at Vence in the early spring of 1930, the miracle was at an end, the flame guttering to extinction. A few days later it was quenched.

Beautiful and absorbingly interesting in themselves, his letters are also of the highest importance as biographical documents. In them, Lawrence has written his life and painted his own portrait. Few men have given more of themselves in their letters. Lawrence is there almost in his entirety. *Almost;* for he obeyed both of Robert Burns's injunctions:

> Aye free, aff han' your story tell,
> When wi' a bosom crony;
> But still keep something to yoursel'
> Ye scarcely tell to ony.

The letters show us Lawrence as he was in his daily living. We see him in all his moods. (And it is curious and amusing to note how his mood will change according to his correspondent. "My kindliness makes me sometimes a bit false," he says of himself severely. In other words, he knew how to adapt himself. To one correspondent he is gay, at moments even larky—because larkiness is expected of him. To another he is gravely reflective. To a third he speaks the language of prophesying and revelation.) We follow him from one vividly seen and recorded landscape to another. We watch him during the war, a subjectivist and a solitary artist, desperately fighting his battle against the nightmare of objective facts and all the inhumanly numerous things that are Caesar's. Fighting and, inevitably, losing. And after the war we accompany him round the world, as he seeks, now in one continent, now in another, some external desert to match the inner wilderness from which he utters his prophetic cry, or some community of which he can feel himself a member. We see him being drawn towards his fellows and then repelled again, making up his mind to force himself into some relation with society and then suddenly changing it again, and letting himself drift once more on the current of circumstances and his own inclinations. And finally, as his illness begins to get the better of him, we see him obscured by a dark cloud of sadness—the terrible sadness, out of which, in one mood, he wrote his savage *Nettles,* in another, *The Man Who Died,* that lovely and profoundly moving story of the miracle for which somewhere in his mind he still hoped—still hoped, against the certain knowledge that it could never happen.

In the earlier part of his career especially, and again towards the end, Lawrence was a most prolific correspondent. There was, however, an intermediate period during his time of wandering, when he seems to have written very little. Of letters with the date of these after-war years, not more than a dozen or two have so far turned up; and there seems to be no reason to believe that further inquiries will reveal the existence of many more. It is not because they have been destroyed or are being withheld that Lawrence's letters of this period are so scarce; it is because, for one reason or another, he did not then care to write letters, that he did not want to feel himself in relationship with anyone. After a time, the stream begins again. But the later letters, though plentiful and good, are neither so numerous nor so richly and variously delightful as the earlier. One feels that Lawrence no longer wanted to give of himself so fully to his correspondents as in the past.

B. R. Haydon

Two likenesses of Haydon hang in the National Portrait Gallery. One, by Miss Zornlin, is a full face, and might be a prophetic portrait of Mussolini. That vast and noble brow, enlarged and ennobled by incipient baldness beyond the limits of verisimilitude; those flashing eyes; that square strong jaw; that wide mouth with its full, floridly sculptured lips; that powerful neck —are not these Il Duce's very features? But Miss Zornlin was not a very good painter. A competent portraitist knows how to imply the profile in the full face. Miss Zornlin's implications are entirely misleading, and if it were not for Haydon's own self-portrait in the National Gallery, and the drawing of him as a youth in the possession of Sir Robert Witt, we should never have guessed that this truculent dictator was the possessor of a very large yet delicately modelled and somehow frail-looking aquiline nose, and a chin which, while not exactly weak, was not so formidably protuberant as one might have expected. It is as though Mussolini had been strangely blended with Cardinal Newman.

From whatever angle one looks at it, the face is remarkable. One would notice it in a crowd; one would know at once that it belonged to some unusual spirit. It is a face that bears the stigmata almost of genius.

[243]

Haydon had only to look in the glass to realize that he was a great man.

Nor was a grand appearance Nature's only gift to him. The other attributes of genius—a little tinged, it is true, with vulgarity—were not lacking. He was endowed with a sharp and comprehensive intelligence; an excellent judgment (except where his own productions were concerned); a daemonic vitality; the proverbial "infinite capacity for taking pains"; a mystical sense of inspiration, and a boundless belief in his own powers. His special gifts were literary and discursive. His brain teemed with general ideas. He was an acute observer of character; he could talk, and he could write. He had a gift of expression, even a literary style. Never was anyone more clearly cut out to be an author. Or, if the outlet of literature had been denied him, he would have made a good politician, a first-rate soldier ("I did not command bayonets and cannons. Would to God," he says himself, "I had!"); he might even—if we may judge from his laborious studies in anatomy and his facility in the propounding of theories—have been a tolerably efficient man of science. The one gift which Nature had quite obviously denied him was the gift of expressing himself in form and colour. One has only to glance at one of Haydon's drawings to perceive that the man had absolutely no artistic talent. The lines are hard, heavy, uncertain and utterly insensitive. He fumbles painfully and blunderingly after likeness to nature, and when he cannot achieve realism falls back on the cheapest art-student tricks. The paintings—such of them, at any rate, as I have seen in the original or in reproductions—are entirely without composition. They abound in bad drawing and disproportions. The colour is crude and inharmonious. In his enormous Agony in the Garden, which now reposes in the cellars of the Victoria and Albert Museum, a shapeless Saviour (straight from the studio and illumined by a strong North light) kneels in the right foreground. Behind Him lies a Rembrandtesque night, full of torch flames, of ruddily illuminated faces and portentous chiaroscuro. The ground is apparently meant to slope up from the place where the Saviour is kneeling. But it slopes in such a curious way that the background seems to be on a level with, if not actually in front of, the figure in the foreground. One is forced to imagine a Mount of Olives constructed like those Tudor houses, in which each storey projects a little farther forward than the one below. The painting is broad, dashing, and ama-teurishly uncertain. In the draperies, and in what is visible of the landscape, one notices great swishing brush strokes entirely devoid of meaning, whole pas-sages daubed in for the sole reason that every inch of the canvas has got to be covered with paint. The thing is ludicrous. The Agony in the Garden is admittedly one of the least successful of Haydon's pictures. I regret that I have never seen his best—Christ's Entry into

Jerusalem, and The Raising of Lazarus. The former is at Cincinnati; to judge by the photographs it bears a certain very distant resemblance to a picture. Where the latter is, I do not know; nor have I ever seen it reproduced. But after having looked at the Agony in the Garden, the portraits at the National Portrait Gallery, and the various reproductions in Sir Robert Witt's library, I feel quite justified in saying that it must be entirely worthless.

Most children are geniuses, and perhaps there may have been some excuse for admiring the scribblings of the infant Haydon. Half the five-year-olds in any country are Raphaels; one in a hundred retains his genius at the age of ten. One in a million of these childish talents survives puberty. Some Imp of the Perverse must have suggested to young Haydon that he was destined to preserve his baby gift and become a painter. Outraged nature protested. The boy was afflicted with a disease of the eyes that permanently weakened his sight. To a natural incapacity to draw or paint was now added an inability to see. It was a broad hint. But the Imp of the Perverse and Haydon's will were very strong. Illness only reinforced the boy's decision to become a painter. All his exuberant energy, which a piece of judicious advice or a happy accident might have harnessed to some congenial labour, was now directed to painting. His self-confidence became a confidence in his powers as an artist. His heavenly muse breathed artistic

inspirations. He had, as he tells us, "perpetual and irresistible urgings of future greatness." And again, "I
have been like a man with air balloons under his arm-
pits and ether in his soul. While I was painting, walking or thinking, beaming flashes of energy followed and
impressed me." To have refused, in such circumstances,
to devote oneself body and soul to painting would have
been the sin against the Holy Ghost. On another occasion, after having "conceived my background stronger
than ever, I strode about the room imitating the
blast of a trumpet—my cheeks full of blood, my heart
beating with a glorious heat. Oh, who would exchange
these moments for a throne?" These ecstatic moments
came to him whenever his mind was occupied with
something that specially interested it. He would spend
a whole evening "in a torrent of feeling about Homer."
On the day after the news of Waterloo had come
through to London, he "got up in a steam of feeling
and read all the papers till he was faint." Since he had
elected painting as the chief concern of his life, it was
natural that these delicious and inspiring moments
came oftenest while he was at work on a picture. They
justified his belief in his own powers, in the same way
as the raptures of the mystic justify his belief in a personal God. An emotion so intense must, it is felt, have
some adequate external cause. Similarly, the sentiments
of a lover are so enormous that it seems impossible that
they should have been aroused by plain Miss Jones or

plainer Mr. Brown. Something cosmic, something divine must have crept in somewhere. Nothing short of the Absolute could account for such ecstasies. A whole literature of platonizing love-poems has arisen, in order that Mr. Robinson's feelings for Miss Smith might be satisfactorily accounted for. Something analogous took place in Haydon's case. Full-blooded, emotional, a sort of Gargantua turned idealistic and romantic, he was easily excited and, when excited, felt profoundly. He could not believe that such prodigious emotions as his were not due to some proportionate cause. If he felt grandly about his painting, that was because his painting was grand, and because to paint was his mission in life, his divinely ordained duty. Of the divine approbation he was, indeed, directly convinced. We find references in the *Autobiography* and Journals to voices which commanded him to embark, even in the midst of financial ruin, on vast and unsaleable works. To his prayers for guidance (and Haydon was always praying) were vouchsafed, so he believed, encouraging replies. And every small success, every happy coincidence—the opportune arrival, for example, of a cheque or a commission—was interpreted by him as a friendly message from the Almighty. It is not to be wondered at if, in the teeth of failure and of hostile criticism, he should have gone on believing in himself. What matter the sneers of human connoisseurs when one *knows*, one is *certain* that the Heavenly Critic approves?

[248]

And then there was Haydon's pride, there was Haydon's ambition. Right or wrong, he had embarked on a painter's career. He was too proud to admit failure and withdraw. And his ambition to excel was inordinate, his vanity was without bounds. He admits (and his frankness is engaging, his perspicacity even in the midst of so much self-deception is remarkable) that he was "always panting for distinction, even at a funeral (for I felt angry at Opie's that I wasn't in the first coach) ." He wanted to be in the first coach at the christening of a new school of English painting. Portrait making, the sham *beau idéal*, petty genre painting were to be ousted from their pre-eminence and historical painting on a colossal scale was to take their place. Haydon was to be the father of the new school. "The production of this picture (Dentatus) must and will be considered an epoch in British Art." And towards the end of his life he records: "I thought once of putting up a brass plate (on his old house in Lisson Grove) , HERE HAYDON PAINTED HIS SOLOMON, 1813."

Sanguine and very susceptible to flattery, Haydon was always ready to believe that the smallest stroke of good fortune must be the herald of complete success, that a word of praise was the first note in that chorus of universal commendation for which he was always anxiously listening. When a "lady of the highest rank" remarked (with that charming and entirely meaningless politeness of which only ladies of the highest rank know the

[249]

secret) : "We look to *you*, Mr. Haydon, to revive the Art," poor Haydon "anticipated all sorts of glory, greatness and fame." He was a man who dramatized his own life, who saw himself acting his own part, not merely as he was playing it at the moment, but in the future too. "I walked about the room, looked into the glass, anticipated what the foreign ambassadors would say, studied my French for a good accent, believed that all the Sovereigns of Europe would hail an English youth who could paint a heroic picture."

The "Sovereigns of Europe," it may be remarked parenthetically, played a great part in Haydon's imaginative life. Of burgess origin, and endowed with a romantic temperament, Haydon was—fatally and inevitably—a snob. The prestige of great names and titles impressed him profoundly. The picturesqueness of traditional aristocracy and the splendours of wealth went violently to his romantic head, just as they went to Balzac's. We have seen how absurdly elated he felt when the "lady of the highest rank" looked to him to "revive the Art." He was as much delighted when Sir George Beaumont and his family "allowed that nothing could exceed the eye of my horse." Even the approbation of a noble savage (if only sufficiently noble) was intoxicating to Haydon, who records complacently that the Persian Ambassador remarked of his Jerusalem "in good English and in a loud voice, 'I like the elbow of soldier.' " But bitter experience soon taught him that

lordly patrons are fickle and their favour not to be relied on. He realized that he had taken their praises of
his historical pictures too seriously. "I forgot," he sadly
remarks, "that the same praise would have been applied
to the portrait of a racehorse or of a favourite pug." He
discovered to his cost that lords and ladies "are am-
bitious of the *éclat* of discovering genius, but their
hearts are seldom engaged for it." And—yet more painful discovery for a man of Haydon's intelligence and
acquirements—"I find the artists most favoured by the
great are those of no education, or those who conceal
what they have. The love of power and superiority is
not trod on if a man of genius is ignorant when a gentleman is informed. 'Great folks,' said Johnson, 'don't
like to have their mouths stopped.'" Haydon was rash
enough to be right about the Elgin Marbles. The great
were all on the side of Payne Knight and grotesquely
wrong. They did not enjoy being told so. But though
he early discovered the truth about aristocratic art patrons—namely, that they regard artists as mere court
fools existing for the entertainment of their endless
leisure, that they take no genuine interest in art, and
are, for the most part, bottomlessly frivolous—though
he knew all this, he yet retained an extraordinary affection and respect for lords. How excessively and abjectly
he enjoys his week-end with Lord Egremont at Petworth! "The very flies at Petworth seem to know that
there is room for their existence, that the windows are

theirs. Dogs, horses, cows, deer and pigs, peasantry and servants, guests and family, children and parents, all share alike his (Lord Egremont's) bounty and opulence and luxury."

He dramatized himself in misfortune no less than in success. It is a fallen Titan who goes to the Debtor's Prison and haggles with creditors. And in spite of everything, how much he enjoys his grandly and dramatically unhappy position at the time when his reforming zeal had made him, in 1832, the official painter of the radical party! At half-past nine he would be in the pawnshop raising money on the silver coffee-pot; at ten he would be sitting in the palace of some peer of the realm, sketching the grand patrician profile and discussing high politics. The afternoon would be spent imploring attorneys to give him time; the evening at some luscious rout where "the beauty of the women, the exquisite, fresh, nose-gay sweetness of their looks, the rich crimson velvet, and white satin, and lace, and muslin, and diamonds, with their black eyes and peachy complexions, and snowy necks, and delicate forms, and graceful motions, and sweet nothingness of conversation bewildered and distracted him." Pauper and pampered pet of society, frequenter of drawing-rooms and pawnshops—the rôle was dramatic, picturesque, positively Shakespearean. He dwells at length, emphatically and almost with pleasure, on his own romantic misery.

Haydon was at all times very conscious of his own

character. He is his own favourite hero of fiction. He
realizes his own energy, genius and vitality, and describes them dramatically in a bold Homeric style. We
find him in his journals constantly comparing himself
to one or other of the nobler animals. He "flies to the
city to raise money, like an eagle." He bathes at Margate "like a bull in June." He is constantly walking up
and down his studio or furiously painting "like a lion."
(And we know from what he says in his journal, after
dissecting one, how much lions meant to Haydon.
"Spent the whole day with a lion and came home with
a contempt for the human species.")

Haydon's belief in himself was infectious, or perhaps
it would be more accurate to say contagious—for it was
only while one was actually in the presence of the
man himself that one could fully believe in his powers
as an artist. In front of his pictures, even his most admiring friends must occasionally have had their doubts.
But the man had such a masterful and magnetic personality, was so large, so exuberantly vital, so intelligent
and plausible, such a good critic of all art but his own,
so well read, such an entertaining talker, that it was
impossible not to take fire at his ardour; it was difficult
when he said, "I am a great artist," not to believe him.
All those, it would be true to say, who came into personal contact with Haydon believed in him. All—from
Keats (who lent him money) and Wordsworth (who addressed two admirable sonnets to him) to the poor wine

merchant, of whom Haydon records "I showed him
Solomon and appealed to him whether I ought, after
such an effort, to be without a glass of wine, which my
medical man had recommended. 'Certainly not,' said
he. 'I'll send you a dozen.'" And he sent them, gratis.
Lamb and Hazlitt and the Hunts were among his
friends and admirers. His landlord, Newton, was infinitely kind to him. His colourman provided him, on
indefinite credit, with canvases of unheard-of dimen-
sions on which to paint unsaleable historical pictures.
Sir Walter Scott not only admired and liked him, but
gave him money. His servant, the faithful Sammons,
seems positively to have worshipped him. There was a
magic about the man, a magic which began to evaporate
as the years passed and a generation arose which had
not known him in his dazzling prime, and the man
himself grew old and querulous and hysterical with
failure and repeated disappointment and chronic poverty. With the final pistol-shot the magic was totally
dissipated. The pictures remain, deplorable monuments
of a wasted life. The real, the magical Haydon can only
be divined from the *Autobiography*.

Haydon was sixty when he committed suicide. One
can only feel astonished that he did not kill himself
before. A few years of the life which Haydon led for
the best part of forty years would have sufficed to drive
most men into suicide, or madness, or the selling of
their principles. Haydon's energy, his sanguine tempera-

ment kept him struggling on, year after year, decade after decade. His later journals make the most distressing reading. In the course of his desperate and never-ending hunt for cash, what agonized anxieties, what humiliations were his daily lot! Familiarity with humiliation seems, indeed, in the long run to have blunted his sensibilities. One has the impression that, after some years of chronic misfortune, it no longer cost him much to write a begging letter or draw up for publication a pathetic statement of his accounts. He was never, even in his early days, very scrupulous about financial matters. The story of his debt to Keats is not told in the *Autobiography*; it must be read in Keats's own letters. It is not, assuredly, very creditable to Haydon. With his usual frankness, Haydon admitted his unscrupulousness about money. "Too proud to do small modest things that I might obtain fair means of existence as I proceeded with my great work, I thought it no degradation to borrow." And again, "I have £400 at Coutts's, thought I, never thinking how I was to return it, but trusting in God for all." Haydon trusted a great deal in God. It salved his conscience to feel that the Almighty was standing security for his I.O.U.'s. But if he was not very honest, he had his justifications. To begin with, he could not afford to be scrupulous. Strict financial honesty is easy only for those whose bank balances are long, or who draw a regular wage and are without ambition. Haydon was filled with vast ambitions, believed himself the greatest painter of his age, and had no money. He felt that the world owed him something for existing, for being the genius that he was. Loans and gifts were received on account of the world's debt to him; he had a certain divine right to them, even when they came from people who could not afford to lend or give. Still he did always honestly try to pay back, later if not sooner, the money he had borrowed. One has only to read the following passage to realize that Haydon had a nice, if peculiar, sense of honour—not to mention a financial ability amounting almost to genius. "In one hour and a half I had ten pounds to pay on my honour and only £2, 15s. in my pocket. I drove away to Newton, paid him £2, 15s. and borrowed £10. I then drove away to my friend and paid him the ten pounds, and borrowed five pounds more, but felt relieved I had not broke my honour."

It must not be thought that Haydon's exertions brought him nothing. First and last, he made considerable sums of money, which might have sufficed to keep a single man in comfort. But Haydon was married. His wife, who was a widow, brought him two small children and no dowry. His own family was numerous. Once every fifty or sixty pages his journals announce a fresh confinement; another little Haydon enters the world. A few years pass, and with a regularity almost as unfailing the little Haydons shuffle off again. One stepson, it is true, reached manhood before he had a promising career in the navy cut short, in the Indian Ocean, by the bite of a sea-serpent. But his case was exceptional. Most of the children died in infancy. After a time one loses count of the births and deaths. I have an impression that about half a dozen children must have survived their father and that about as many died before they were six years old. Perhaps if one hunted among the sooty grasses of Paddington Green, in the shadow of Mrs. Siddons's monument, one might still find their little tombstones.

Haydon was a most conscientious father—rather too conscientious, considering that he could not possibly afford to educate his children as aristocratically as he did. Some of the most pressing debts of his later years were for his sons' tutorial and college dues at Oxford and Cambridge.

Towards the end of his life Haydon was no longer too proud to do "small modest things." His ambition was still to paint huge historical pictures; but meanwhile, to keep the pot boiling, he was prepared to stoop to a pettier kind of art. He painted portraits—that is, when he could find sitters. But he hated portrait painting. Lacking, as he did, any understanding of, or interest in, the formal side of art, he could never paint for painting's sake. He was only interested in the literature of painting; he needed a subject to stimulate his imagination. "In portrait," he complains, "I lose that divine feeling of inspiration which I always had in his-

tory. I feel a common man." What he really liked
painting was something in the style of The Plagues
of Egypt. "A Sphinx or two, a pyramid or so, with the
front groups lighted by torches, would make this a
subject terrific and appalling." There was nothing very
terrific or appalling about the stout business men and
their wives and ugly daughters who came to have their
portraits painted at twenty-five or thirty pounds a time.
Moreover, Haydon was, as he himself admits, a very bad
portrait painter. He soon lost whatever patronage he
had. He felt the loss as something of a relief.

More congenial, at any rate to begin with, and no
less lucrative than portraits, were his fancy pictures of
Napoleon musing. Haydon's first picture of Napoleon
on St. Helena caught the public fancy. It represents
the Emperor standing on a crag, with his back to the
spectator, contemplating the Atlantic Ocean, the remains of a sunset and the crescent moon. The piece
was engraved and sold well. Sir Robert Peel bought the
original. Replicas were ordered in quantities. For years
Haydon lived on Napoleon musing—musing, not
merely on St. Helena, but at Fontainebleau, in his bedroom, on the ocean, at Marengo, in Egypt before the
pyramids. He turned them out by the dozen. Haydon
also painted a picture of the Duke of Wellington musing on the field of Waterloo; but the piece was much
less successful. Perhaps it was felt that the picture
lacked verisimilitude. French tyrants might muse; but

not an English general, not a Wellesley, a Duke, a Prime Minister.

Haydon's self-confidence remained apparently unshaken to the end. Indeed, as failure was heaped upon failure, disappointment on disappointment, it expressed itself more vehemently than ever, with a kind of shrill, hysterical defiance. After the rejection of the cartoons which he had prepared for the decoration of the new Houses of Parliament—the cruellest blow of Haydon's whole unhappy career—he tried to comfort himself by insisting with an almost insane violence on his own genius. "What magic! what fire! what unerring hand and eye! what a gift of God! I bow and am grateful." And looking at his Solomon ("this wonderful picture") he asks himself: "Ought I to fear comparison of it with the Duke of Sutherland's Murillo, or any other picture?" And he answers with a confidence that would be ludicrous if it were not painfully pathetic, "Certainly not!" At this period, too, he liked to insist more strongly than ever on the altruistic, the self-sacrificingly patriotic character of his whole career. He had always claimed that he was working for the glory of British Art. By the end of his life he was saying that he "had devoted himself without a selfish feeling to the honour of his country." The sense that he was a martyr to a great cause gave him, no doubt, a certain comfort in his misery.

His religion was another source of comfort. His journals reveal him in close and constant communication with his Maker. There is something curiously primitive about his prayers. He asks for specific material benefits, for the providential and almost miraculous solution of particular difficulties. This is how he prepares for one of his exhibitions: "Grant, during the exhibition, nothing may happen to dull its success, but that it may go on in one continuous stream of triumphant success to the last instant. O God, thou knowest I am in the clutches of a villain; grant me the power to get out of them, for Jesus Christ's sake. Amen. And subdue the evil disposition of that villain, so that I may extricate myself from his power without getting further into it." (An only too accurate description of Haydon's ordinary method of paying off debts.) "Grant this for Jesus Christ's sake. Amen, with all my soul." The prayer, alas, was not answered. On the day that Haydon opened his exhibition, Barnum arrived in town with General Tom Thumb. Unconsciously cruel, he hired a room in the Egyptian Hall next to Haydon's. Standing at the door of his empty gallery, the unhappy artist could watch the crowds that surged and shoved and fought in a Gadarene scramble to see the dwarf.

But enough of misery and failure and incompetence. Haydon was something more than a bad and deservedly unsuccessful painter. He was a great personality to begin with. And in the second place he was, as I like to think, a born writer who wasted his life making absurd pictures when he might have been making excellent books. One book, however, he did contrive to make. The *Autobiography* reveals his powers. Reading it, one realizes the enormity of that initial mistake which sent him from his father's bookshop to the Academy schools. As a romantic novelist what might he not have achieved? Sadly one speculates.

There were times when Haydon himself seems to have speculated even as we do. "The truth is," he remarks near the end of his life, "I am fonder of books than of anything else on earth. I consider myself, and ever shall, a man of great powers, excited to an art which limits their exercise. In politics, law or literature they would have had a full and glorious swing. . . . It is a curious proof of this that I have pawned my studies, my prints, my lay figures, but have kept my darling authors." The avowal is complete. What genuine, born painter would call painting an art which limits the exercise of great powers? Such a criticism could only come from a man to whom painting was but another and less effectual way of writing dramas, novels or history.

It is, I repeat, as a novelist that Haydon would best have exhibited his powers. I can imagine great rambling books in which absured sublimities ("a Sphinx or two, a pyramid or so") and much rhapsodical philosophizing would have alternated in the approved Shakespearean or Faustian style, with admirable passages of well-observed, naturalistic comic relief. We should yawn over the philosophy and perhaps smile at the sublimities (as we smile and yawn even at Byron's; who can now read *Manfred*, or *Cain*?) ; but we should eagerly devour the comic chapters. The *Autobiography* permits us to imagine how good these chapters might have been.

Haydon was an acute observer, and he knew how to tell a story. How vividly, for example, he has seen this tea-party at Mrs. Siddons's, how well he has described it! "After her first reading (from Shakespeare) the men retired to tea. While we were all eating toast and tingling cups and saucers, she began again. It was like the effect of a Mass bell at Madrid. All noise ceased, we slunk to our seats like boors, two or three of the most distinguished men of the day with the very toast in their mouths, afraid to bite. It was curious to see Lawrence in this predicament, to hear him bite by degrees and then stop, for fear of making too much crackle, his eyes full of water from the constraint; and at the same time to hear Mrs. Siddons's 'eye of newt and toe of frog,' and then to see Lawrence give a sly bite and then look awed and pretend to be listening. I went away highly gratified and as I stood on the landing-place to get cool, I overheard my own servant in the hall say, 'What! is that the old lady making such a noise?' 'Yes.' 'Why, she makes as much noise as ever.' 'Yes,' was the answer, 'she tunes her pipes as well as ever she did.' " There are, in the *Autobiography*, scores of such admirable little narratives and descriptions.

Haydon's anecdotes about the celebrated men with whom he came in contact are revealing as well as entertaining. They prove that he had more than a memory, a sense of character, an instinctive feeling for the significant detail. Most of the anecdotes are well known and have often been reprinted. But I cannot resist quoting two little stories about Wordsworth, which are less celebrated than they deserve to be. One day Haydon and Wordsworth went together to an art gallery. "In the corner stood the group of Cupid and Psyche kissing. After looking some time, he turned round to me with an expression I shall never forget, and said, 'The Dev-ils!' " From this one anecdote a subtle psychologist might almost have divined the youthful escapade in France, the illegitimate daughter, the subsequent remorse and respectability. The other story is hardly less illuminating. "One day Wordsworth at a large party leaned forward in a moment of silence and said: 'Davy, do you know the reason I published my "White Doe" in quarto?' 'No,' said Davy, slightly blushing at the attention this awakened. 'To express my own opinion of it,' replied Wordsworth."

Merely as a verbal technician Haydon was singularly gifted. When he is writing about something which deeply interests and excites him, his style takes on a florid and violent brilliance all its own. For example, this is how, at the coronation of George IV, he describes the royal entrance. "Three or four of high rank appear from behind the throne; an interval is left; the crowd scarce breathe. Something rustles; and a being buried in satin, feathers and diamonds rolls gracefully into his seat. The room rises with a sort of feathered, silken thunder." He knows how to use his adjectives with admirable effect. The most accomplished writer might envy his description of the Duke of Sussex's voice as "loud, royal and asthmatic." And how one shudders at the glance of a "tremendous, globular and demoniacal eye!" How one loves the waitresses at the eating-house where the young and always susceptible Haydon used to dine! When they heard that he was bankrupt, these "pretty girls eyed me with a lustrous regret."

Haydon could argue with force and clarity. He could be witty as well as floridly brilliant. The man who could talk of Charles Lamb "stuttering his quaintness in snatches, like the Fool in *Lear*, and with as much beauty," certainly knew how to turn a phrase. He could imply a complete criticism in a dozen words; when he has said of West's classical pictures that "the Venuses looked as though they had never been naked before," there is nothing more to add; the last word on neoclassicism has been uttered. And what a sound, what a neatly pointed comment on English portrait painting is contained in the following brief sentences! "Portraiture is always independent of art and has little or nothing to do with it. It is one of the staple manufactures of the Empire. Wherever the British settle, wherever they colonize, they carry, and will ever carry, trial by jury, horse-racing and portrait painting." And let us hope they will ever carry a good supply of those indomitable madmen who have made the British Empire and English literature, English politics and English science the extraordinary things they are. Haydon was one of these glorious lunatics. An ironic fate decreed that he should waste his madness in the practice of an art for which he was not gifted. But though wasted, the insanity was genuine and of good quality. The *Autobiography* makes us wish that it might have been better directed.

Waterworks and Kings

IN THE chancelleries of eighteenth-century Europe nobody bothered very much about Hesse. Its hostility was not a menace, its friendship brought no positive advantages. Hesse was only one of the lesser German states—a tenth-rate Power.

Tenth-rate: and yet, on the outskirts of Kassel, which was the capital of this absurdly unimportant principality, there stands a palace large and splendid enough to house a full-blown emperor. And from the main façade of this palace there rises to the very top of the neighbouring mountain one of the most magnificent architectural gardens in the world. This garden, which is like a straight wide corridor of formal stone-work driven through the hillside forest, climbs up to a nondescript building in the grandest Roman manner, almost as large as a cathedral and surmounted by a colossal bronze statue of Hercules. Between Hercules at the top and the palace at the bottom lies an immense series of terraces, with fountains and cascades, pools, grottos, spouting tritons, dolphins, nereids and all the other mythological fauna of an eighteenth-century water-garden. The spectacle, when the waters are flowing, is magnificent. There must be the best part of two miles of neo-classic cataract and elegantly canalized foam. The waterworks at Versailles are tame and trivial in comparison.

It was Whit Sunday when I was at Kassel. With almost the entire population of the town I had climbed up to the shrine of Hercules on the hilltop. Standing there in the shadow of the god, with the waters in full splash below me and the sunshine brilliant on the green dome of the palace at the long cataract's foot, I found myself prosaically speculating about ways and means and motives. How could a mere prince of Hesse run to such imperial splendours? And why, having somehow raised the money, should he elect to spend it in so fantastically wasteful a fashion? And, finally, why did the Hessians ever put up with his extravagance? The money, after all, was theirs; seeing it all squandered on a house and a garden, why didn't they rise up against their silly, irresponsible tyrant?

The answer to these last questions was being provided, even as I asked them, by the good citizens of Kassel around me. *Schön, herrlich, prachtvoll*—their admiration exploded emphatically on every side. Without any doubt, they were thoroughly enjoying themselves. In six generations, humanity cannot undergo any fundamental change. There is no reason to suppose that the Hessians of 1750 were greatly different from those of 1932. Whenever the prince allowed his subjects to visit his waterworks, they came and, I have no doubt, admired and enjoyed their admiration just as much as their descendants do to-day. The psychology of revolutionaries is apt to be a trifle crude. The magnificent display of wealth does not necessarily, as they imagine, excite a passion of envy in the hearts of the poor. Given a reasonable amount of prosperity, it excites, more often, nothing but pleasure. The Hessians did not rise up and kill their prince for having wasted so much money on his house and garden; on the contrary, they were probably grateful to him for having realized in solid stone and rainbow-flashing water their own vague day-dreams of a fairy-tale magnificence. One of the functions of royalty is to provide people with a vicarious, but none the less real, fulfilment of their wishes. Kings who make a fine show are popular; and the people not only forgive, but actually commend, extravagances which, to the good Marxian, must seem merely criminal. Wise kings always earmarked a certain percentage of their income for display. Palaces and waterworks were good publicity for kingship, just as an impressive office building is good publicity for a business corporation. Business, indeed, has inherited many of the responsibilities of royalty. It shares with the State and the municipality the important duty of providing the common people with vicarious wish-fulfilments. Kings no longer build palaces; but newspapers and insurance companies do. Popular restaurants are as richly marbled as the mausoleum of the Escorial; hotels are more splendid than Versailles. In every society there must always be some person or some organization whose task it is to realize the day-dreams of the masses. Life in a perfectly sensible, utilitarian community would be intolerably dreary. Occasional explosions of magnificent folly are as essential to human well-being as a sewage system. More so, probably. Sanitary plumbing, it is significant to note, is a very recent invention; the splendours of kingship are as old as civilization itself.

In a Tunisian Oasis

WAKING at dawn, I looked out of the window. We were in the desert. On either side of the railway an immense plain, flat as Holland, but tawny instead of green, stretched out interminably. On the horizon, instead of windmills, a row of camels was silhouetted against the grey sky. Mile after mile, the train rolled slowly southward.

At Tozeur, when at last we arrived, it had just finished raining—for the first time in two and a half years—and now the wind had sprung up; there was a sandstorm. A thick brown fog, whirled into eddies by the wind, gritty to the skin, abolished the landscape from before our smarting eyes. We sneezed; there was sand in our ears, in our hair, between our teeth. It was horrible. I felt depressed, but not surprised. The weather is always horrible when I travel.

Once, in a French hotel, I was accused of having brought with me the flat black bugs, of whose presence among my bed-clothes I complained to a self righteous proprietress. I defended myself with energy against the impeachment. Bugs—no; I am innocent of bugs. But when it comes to bad weather, I have to plead guilty. Rain, frost, wind, snow, hail, fog—I bring them with me wherever I go. I bring them to places where they have never been heard of, at seasons when it is impossible that they should occur. What delightful skating there will be in the Spice Islands when I arrive! On this particular journey I had brought with me to every place on my itinerary the most appalling meteorological calamities. At Naples, for example, it was the snow. Coming out of the theatre on the night of our arrival, we found it lying an inch deep under the palm trees in the public gardens. And Vesuvius, next morning, glittered white, like Fujiyama, against the pale spring sky. At Palermo there was a cloud-burst. "Between the Syrtes and soft Sicily" we passed through a tempest of hail, lightning and wind. At Tunis it very nearly froze. At Sousse the wind was so violent that the stiff board-like leaves of the cactuses swayed and trembled in the air like aspens. And now, on the day of our arrival at Tozeur, it had rained for the first time in thirty months, and there was a sandstorm. No, I was not in the least surprised; but I could not help feeling a little gloomy.

Towards evening the wind somewhat abated; the sand began to drop out of the air. At midday the brown curtain had been impenetrable at fifty yards. It thinned, grew gauzier; one could see objects at a hundred, two hundred yards. From the windows of the hotel bedroom in which we had sat all day, trying—but in vain, for it came through even invisible crannies—to escape from the wind-blown sand, we could see the fringes of a dense forest of palm trees, the dome of a little mosque,

[271]

houses of sun-dried brick and thin brown men in flapping nightshirts walking, with muffled faces and bent heads, against the wind, or riding, sometimes astride, sometimes sideways, on the bony rumps of patient little asses. Two very professional tourists in sun helmets —there was no sun—emerged round the corner of a street. A malicious gust of wind caught them unawares; simultaneously the two helmets shot into the air, thudded, rolled in the dust. The too professional tourists scuttled in pursuit. The spectacle cheered us a little; we descended, we ventured out of doors.

A melancholy Arab offered to show us round the town. Knowing how hard it is to find one's way in these smelly labyrinths, we accepted his offer. His knowledge of French was limited; so too, in consequence, was the information he gave us. He employed what I may call the Berlitz method. Thus, when a column of whirling sand rose up and jumped at us round the corner of a street, our guide turned to us and said, pointing: *"Poussière."* We might have guessed it ourselves.

He led us interminably through narrow, many-cornered streets between eyeless walls, half crumbled and tottering.

"Village," he explained. *"Très plaisant."* We did not altogether agree with him.

A walk through an Arab village is reminiscent of walks through Ostia or Pompeii. Roman remains are generally in a better state of preservation, and cleaner;

that is all. One is astonished to see, among these dusty ruins, white-robed families crouching over their repasts.

Our guide patted a brown mud wall.

"*Briques,*" he said, and repeated the word several times, so that we might be certain what he meant.

These bricks, which are of sun-dried mud, are sometimes, on the façades of the more considerable houses, arranged in a series of simple and pleasing patterns— diamonds, quincunxes, hexagons. A local art which nobody now takes the trouble to practise—nobody, that is, except the Europeans, who, with characteristic energy, have used and wildly abused the traditional ornamentation on the walls of the station and the principal hotel. It is a curious and characteristic fact that, whenever in Tunisia one sees a particularly Oriental piece of architecture, it is sure to have been built by the French, since 1881. The cathedral of Carthage, the law courts and schools of Tunis—these are more Moorish than the Alhambra, Moorish as only Oriental tea-rooms in Paris or London can be Moorish. In thirty years the French have produced buildings more typically and intensely Arabian than the Arabs themselves contrived to do in the course of thirteen centuries.

We passed into the market-place.

"*Viande,*" said our guide, fingering as he passed a

well-thumbed collop of mutton, lying among the dust and flies on a little booth.

We nodded.

"*Très joli,*" commented our guide. "*Très plaisant.*" Noisily he spat on the ground. The proprietor of the booth spat too. We hurried away; it needs time to grow inured to Tunisian habits. These frightful hoickings in the throat, these sibilant explosions and semi-liquid impacts are almost the national music of the country.

There are in the desert of southern Tunisia three great oases: Gabes by the sea, a little north of that island of Djerba which is, traditionally, the classical Island of the Lotus Eaters; Tozeur, to the west of it, some seventy miles inland; and Nefta, fifteen miles west of Tozeur, the starting-point of the caravans which trade between southern Tunisia and the great oases of the Algerian Sahara, Biskra and Touggourt. These oases are all of much the same size, each consisting of some six or seven thousand acres of cultivated ground, and are all three remarkable for their numerous and copious springs. In the middle of the desert, suddenly, a hundred fountains come welling out of the sand; rivers run, a network of little canals is dug. An innumerable forest of date palms springs up—a forest whose undergrowth is corn and roses, vines and apricot trees, olives and pomegranates, pepper trees, castor-oil trees, banana trees, every precious plant of the temperate and the subtropical zones. No rain falls on these little Edens—except on the days of my arrival—but the springs, fed from who knows what distant source, flow inexhaustibly and have flowed at least since Roman times. Islanded among the sands, their green luxuriance is a standing miracle. That it should have been in a desert, with here and there such islands of palm trees, that Judaism and Mohammedanism took their rise is a thing which, since I have seen an oasis, astonishes me. The religion which, in such a country, would naturally suggest itself to me would be no abstract monotheism, but the adoration of life, of the forces of green and growing nature. In an oasis, it seems to me, the worship of Pan and of the Great Mother should be celebrated with an almost desperate earnestness. The nymphs of water and of trees ought surely, here, to receive a passionate gratitude. In the desert, I should infallibly have invented the Greek mythology. The Jews and the Arabs discovered Jahweh and Allah. I find it strange.

Of the three great Tunisian oases, my favourite is Nefta. Gabes runs it close for beauty, while the proximity of the sea gives it a charm which Nefta lacks. But, on the other hand, Gabes is less fertile than Nefta and, socially, more sophisticated. There must be the best part of two hundred Europeans living at Gabes. There is dancing once a week at the hotel. Gabes is quite the little Paris. The same objection applies to Tozeur, which has a railway station and positively teems with French officials. Nefta, with fourteen thousand Arabs, has a white population of a dozen or thereabouts. A hundred Frenchman can always make a Paris; twelve, I am happy to say, cannot. The only non-Arabian feature of Nefta is its hotel, which is clean, comfortable, French and efficient. At Nefta one may live among barbarians, in the Middle Ages, and at the same time, for thirty francs a day, enjoy the advantages of contemporary Western civilization. What could be more delightful?

We set off next morning by car, across the desert. From Tozeur the road mounts slightly to a plateau which dominates the surrounding country. The day was clear and sunny. We looked down on the green island of Tozeur—four hundred thousand palm trees among the sands. Beyond the oasis we could see the chotts, glittering in the sun. The chotts are shallow depressions in the ground, at one time, no doubt, the beds of considerable lakes. There is no water in them now; but the soil is furred with a bright saline efflorescence. At a distance, you could swear you saw the sea. For the rest, the landscape was all sand and lion-coloured rock.

We bumped on across the desert. Every now and then we passed a camel, a string of camels. Their owners walked or rode on asses beside them. The womenfolk were perched among the baggage on the hump—a testimony, most eloquent in this Mohammedan country, to the great discomfort of camel riding. Once we met a small Citroën lorry, crammed to overflowing with white-robed Arabs. In the Sahara, the automobile has begun to challenge the supremacy of the camel. Little ten-horse-power Citroëns dart about the desert. For the rougher mountainous country special six-wheeled cars are needed, and with caterpillar wheels one may even affront the soft and shifting sand of the dunes. Motor buses now ply across the desert. A line, we were told, was shortly to be inaugurated between Nefta and Touggourt, across two hundred kilometres of sand. In a few years, no doubt, we shall all have visited Lake Tchad and Timbuctoo. Should one be glad or sorry? I find it difficult to decide.

The hotel at Nefta is a long low building, occupying one whole side of the market-square. From your bedroom window you watch the Arabs living; they do it unhurriedly and with a dignified inefficiency. Endlessly haggling, they buy and sell. The vendor offers a mutton chop, slightly soiled; the buyer professes himself outraged by a price which would be exorbitant if the goods were spotlessly first-hand. It takes them half an hour to come to a compromise. On the ground white bundles doze in the sun; when the sun grows too hot, they roll a few yards and doze again in the shade. The notables of the town, the rich proprietors of palm trees, stroll past with the dignity of Roman senators. Their garments are of the finest wool; they carry walking sticks; they wear European shoes and socks, and on their bare brown calves—a little touch entirely characteristic of the real as opposed to the literary East—pale mauve or shell-pink sock suspenders. Wild men ride in from the desert. Some of them, trusting to common sense as well as Allah to preserve them from ophthalmia, wear smoked motor goggles. With much shouting, much reverberant thumping of dusty, moth-eaten hides, a string of camels is driven in. They kneel, they are unloaded. Supercilious and haughty, they turn this way and that, like the dowagers of very aristocratic families at a plebeian evening party. Then, all at once, one of them stretches out its long neck limply along the ground and shuts its eyes. The movement is one of hopeless weariness; the grotesque animal is suddenly pathetic. And what groanings, what gurglings in the throat, what enormous sighs when their masters begin to reload them! Every additional package evokes a bubbling protest, and when at last they have to rise from their knees, they moan as though their hearts were broken. Blind beggars sit patiently awaiting the alms they never receive. Their raw eyelids black with flies, small children play contentedly in the dust. If Allah wills it, they too will be blind one day: blessed be the name of Allah.

Sitting at our window, we watch the spectacle. And at night, after a pink and yellow sunset with silhouetted palm trees and domes against the sky (for my taste, I am afraid, altogether too like the coloured plates in

the illustrated Bible), at night huge stars come out in
the indigo sky, the cafés are little caves of yellow light,
draped figures move in the narrow streets with lanterns
in their hands, and on the flat roofs of the houses one
sees the prowling shadows of enormous watch-dogs.
There is silence, the silence of the desert: from time
to time there comes to us, very distinctly, the distant
sound of spitting.

Walking among the crowds of the market-place or
along the narrow labyrinthine streets, I was always
agreeably surprised by the apathetically courteous aloof-
ness of Arab manners. It had been the same in Tunis
and the other larger towns. It is only by Jews and
Europeanized Arabs that the tourist is pestered: through
the native quarters he walks untroubled. There are
beggars in plenty, of course, hawkers, guides, cab drivers; and when you pass, they faintly stir, it is true, from
their impassive calm. They stretch out hands, they offer
Arab antiquities of the most genuine German manu-
facture, they propose to take you the round of the
sights, they invite you into their fly-blown vehicles. But
they do all these things politely and quite uninsistently.
A single refusal suffices to check their nascent importunity. You shake your head; they relapse once more
into the apathy from which your appearance momentarily roused them—resignedly: nay almost, you feel,
with a sense of relief that it had not, after all, been
necessary to disturb themselves. Coming from Naples,

[279]

we had been particularly struck by this lethargic politeness. For in Naples the beggars claim an alms noisily
and as though by right. If you refuse to ride, the cab-
men of Pozzuoli follow you up the road, alternately
cursing and whining, and at every hundred yards reducing their price by yet another ten per cent. The
guides at Pompeii fairly insist on being taken; they
cry aloud, they show their certificates, they enumerate
their wives and starving children. As for the hawkers,
they simply will not let you go. What, you don't want
coloured photographs of Vesuvius? Then look at these
corals. No corals? But here is the last word in cigarette
holders. You do not smoke? But in any case, you shave;
these razor blades, now . . . You shake your head.
Then toothpicks, magnifying glasses, celluloid combs.
Stubbornly, you continue to refuse. The hawker plays
his last card—an ace, it must be admitted, and of
trumps. He comes very close to you, he blows garlic
and alcohol confidentially into your face. From an inner
pocket he produces an envelope; he opens it, he presses
the contents into your hand. You may not want corals
or razor blades, views of Vesuvius or celluloid combs;
he admits it. But can you honestly say—honestly, with
your hand on your heart—that you have no use for
pornographic engravings? And for nothing, sir, positively for nothing. Ten francs apiece; the set of twelve
for a hundred. . . .

The touts, the pimps, the mendicants of Italy are the

energetic members of a conquering, progressive race. The Neapolitan cabman is a disciple of Samuel Smiles; the vendors of pornographic post cards and the sturdy beggars live their lives with a strenuousness that would have earned the commendation of a Roosevelt. Self-help and the strenuous life do not flourish on the other shore of the Mediterranean. In Tunisia the tourist walks abroad unpestered. The Arabs have no future.

And yet there were periods in the past when the Arabs were a progressing people. During the centuries which immediately followed Mohammed's apostolate, the Arabs had a future—a future and a most formidable present. Too much insistence on the fatalism inherent in their religion has reduced them to the condition of static lethargy and supine incuriousness in which they now find themselves. That they might still have a future if they changed their philosophy of life must be obvious to anyone who has watched the behaviour of Arab children, who have not yet had time to be influenced by the prevailing fatalism of Islam. Arab children are as lively, as inquisitive, as tiresome and as charming as the children of the most progressively Western people. At Nefta the adult beggars and donkey drivers might leave us, resignedly, in peace; but the children were unescapable. We could never stir abroad without finding a little troop of them frisking around us. It was in vain that we tried to drive them away; they accompanied us, whether we liked it or no,

[281]

on every walk, and, when the walk was over, claimed wages for their importunate fidelity.

To provide tourists with guidance they did not need —this, we found, was the staple profession of the little boys of Nefta. But they had other and more ingenious ways of making money. Close and acute observers of tourists, they had made an important psychological discovery about this curious race of beings. Foreigners, they found out, especially elderly female foreigners, have a preposterous tenderness for animals. The little boys of Nefta have systematically exploited this discovery. Their methods, which we had frequent opportunities of observing, are simple and effective. In front of the hotel a gang of little ruffians is perpetually on the watch. A tourist shows himself, or herself, on one of the balconies; immediately the general of the troop— or perhaps it would be better to call him the director of the company, for it is obvious that the whole affair is organized on a strictly business footing—runs forward to within easy coin-tossing distance. From somewhere about his person he produces a captive bird—generally some brightly coloured little creature not unlike a goldfinch. Smiling up at the tourist, he shows his prize. *"Oiseau,"* he explains in his pidgin French. When the tourist has been made to understand that the bird is alive, the little boy proceeds, with the elaborate gestures of a conjurer, to pretend to wring its neck, to pull off its legs and wings, to pluck out its feathers. For a tender-hearted tourist the menacing pantomime is unbearable.

"Lâche la bête. Je te donne dix sous."

Released, the bird flaps ineffectually away, as well as its clipped wings will permit. The coins are duly thrown and in the twinkling of an eye picked up. And the little boys scamper off to recapture the feebly fluttering source of their income. After seeing an old English lady blackmailed out of a small fortune for the ten-times-repeated release of a single captive, we hardened our hearts whenever birds were produced for our benefit. The little boys went through the most elaborately savage mimcry. We looked on calmly. In actual fact, we observed, they never did their victims any harm. A bird, it was obvious, was far too valuable to be lightly killed; goldfinches during the tourist season laid golden eggs. Besides, they were really very nice little boys and fond of their pets. When they saw that we had seen through their trick and could not be induced to pay ransom, they grinned up at us without malice and knowingly, as though we were their accomplices, and carefully put the birds away.

The importunity of the little boys was tiresome when one wanted to be alone. But if one happened to be in the mood for it, their company was exceedingly entertaining. The exploitation of the tourists was a monopoly which the most active of the children had arrogated, by force and cunning, to themselves. There was

a little gang of them who shared the loot and kept
competitors at a distance. By the time we left, we had
got to know them very well. When we walked abroad,
small strangers tried to join our party; but they were
savagely driven away with shouts and blows. We were
private property; no trespassing was tolerated. It was
only by threatening to stop their wages that we could
persuade the captains of the Nefta tourist industry to
desist from persecuting their rivals. There was one
particularly charming little boy—mythically beautiful,
as only Arab children can be beautiful—who was the
object of their special fury. The captains of the tourist industry were ugly: they dreaded the rivalry of this
lovely child. And they were right; he was irresistible.
We insisted on his being permitted to accompany us.

"But why do you send him away?" we asked.

"*Lui méchant,*" the captains of industry replied in
their rudimentary French. "*Lui casser un touriste.*"

"He smashed a tourist?" we repeated in some astonishment.

They nodded. Blushing, even the child himself
seemed reluctantly to admit the truth of their accusa-
tions. We could get no further explanations; none of
them knew enough French to give them. "*Lui méchant. Lui casser un touriste.*" That was all we could
discover. The lovely child looked at us appealingly.
We decided to run the risk of being smashed and let

him come with us. I may add that we came back from all our walks quite intact.

Under the palm trees, through that labyrinth of paths and running streams, we wandered interminably with our rabble of little guides. Most often it was to that part of the oasis called the *Corbeille* that we went. At the bottom of a rounded valley, theatre-shaped and with smooth steep sides of sand, a score of springs suddenly gush out. There are little lakes, jade green like those pools beneath the cypresses of the Villa d'Este at Tivoli. Round their borders the palm trees go jetting up, like fountains fixed in their upward aspiring gesture, their drooping crown of leaves a green spray arrested on the point of falling. Fountains of life—and five yards away the smooth unbroken slopes of sand glare in the sun. A little river flows out from the lakes, at first between high banks, then into an open sheet of water where the children paddle and bathe, the beasts come down to drink, the women do their washing. The river is the main road in this part of the oasis. The Arabs, when they want to get from place to place, tuck up their night-shirts and wade. Shoes and stockings, not to mention the necessity for keeping up their dignified prestige, do not permit Europeans to follow their example. It is only on mule-back that Europeans use the river road. On foot, with our little guides, we had to scramble precariously on the slopes of crumbling banks, to go balancing across bridges made of a single palm stem, to overleap the mud walls of gardens. The owners of these gardens had a way of making us indirectly pay toll for our passage across their property. Politely, they asked us if we would like a drink of palm wine. It was impossible to say no; we protested that we should be delighted. With the agility of a monkey, a boy would fairly run up a palm tree, to bring down with him a little earthenware pot full of the sap which flows from an incision made for the purpose at the top of the stem, in the centre of the crown of leaves. The pot, never too scrupulously clean, was offered to us; we had to drink, or at least pretend to drink, a horribly sickly fluid tasting of sugared water slightly flavoured with the smell of fresh cabbage leaves. One was happy to pay a franc or two to be allowed to return the stuff untasted to the owner. I may add here that none of the drinks indigenous to Nefta are satisfactory. The palm juice makes one sick, the milk is rather goaty, and the water is impregnated with magnesia, has a taste of Carlsbad or Hunyadi Janos, and produces on all but hardened drinkers of it the same physiological effects as do the waters of those more celebrated springs. There is no alternative but wine. And fortunately Tunisia is rich in admirable vintages. The red wines of Carthage are really delicious, and even the smallest of *vins ordinaires* are very drinkable.

A fertile oasis possesses a characteristic colour scheme of its own, which is entirely unlike that of any landscape in Italy or the north. The fundamental note is struck by the palms. Their foliage, except where the stiff shiny leaves metallically reflect the light, is a rich blue-green. Beneath them, one walks in a luminous aquarium shadow, broken by innumerable vivid shafts of sunlight that scatter gold over the ground or, touching the trunks of the palm trees, make them shine a pale ashy pink through the subaqueous shadow. There is pink, too, in the glaring whiteness of the sand beyond the fringes of the oasis. Under the palms, beside the brown or jade-coloured water, glows the bright emerald green of corn or the deciduous trees of the north, with here and there the huge yellowish leaves of a banana tree, the smoky grey of olives, or the bare bone-white and writhing form of a fig tree.

As the sun gradually sinks, the aquarium shadow beneath the palm trees grows bluer, denser; you imagine yourself descending through layer after darkening layer of water. Only the pale skeletons of the fig trees stand out distinctly; the waters gleam like eyes in the dark ground; the ghost of a little marabout or chapel shows its domed silhouette, white and strangely definite in the growing darkness, through a gap in the trees. But looking up from the depths of this submarine twilight, one sees the bright pale sky of evening, and against it, still touched by the level, rosily-golden light, gleaming as though transmuted into sheets of precious metal, the highest leaves of the palm trees.

A little wind springs up; the palm leaves rattle together; it is suddenly cold. *"En avant,"* we call. Our little guides quicken their pace. We follow them through the darkening mazes of the palm forest, out into the open. The village lies high on the desert plateau above the oasis, desert-coloured, like an arid outcrop of the tawny rock. We mount to its nearest gate. Through passage-ways between blank walls, under long dark tunnels the children lead us—an obscure and tortuous way which we never succeeded in thoroughly mastering—back to the square market-place at the centre of the town. The windows of the inn glimmer invitingly. At the door we pay off the captains of industry and the little tourist-smasher; we enter. Within the hotel it is provincial France.

For longer expeditions entailing the use of mules or asses, we had to take grown-up guides. They knew almost as little French as the children, and their intelligence was wrapped impenetrably in the folds of fatalism. Talking to an Islamically educated Arab is like talking to a pious European of the fourteenth century. Every phenomenon is referred by them to its final cause—to God. About the immediate causes of things—precisely how they happen—they seem to feel not the slightest interest. Indeed, it is not even admitted that there are such things as immediate causes: God is directly responsible for everything.

"Do you think it will rain?" you ask, pointing to menacing clouds overhead.

"If God wills," is the answer.

You pass the native hospital. "Are the doctors good?"

"In our country," the Arab gravely replies, in the tone of Solomon, "we say that doctors are of no avail. If Allah wills that a man shall die, he will die. If not, he will recover."

All of which is profoundly true, so true, indeed, that it is not worth saying. To the Arab, however, it seems the last word in human wisdom. For him, God is the perfectly adequate explanation of everything; he leaves fate to do things unassisted, in its own way—that is to say, from the human point of view, the worst way.

It is difficult for us to realize nowadays that our fathers once thought much as the Arabs do now. As late as the seventeenth century, the chemist Boyle found it necessary to protest against what I may call this Arabian view of things.

"For to explicate a phenomenon," he wrote, "it is not enough to ascribe it to one general efficient, but we must intelligibly show the particular manner, how that general cause produces the proposed effect. He must be a very dull inquirer who, demanding an account of the phenomena of a watch, shall rest satisfied with being told that it is an engine made by a watchmaker; though nothing be declared thereby of the structure and coaptation of the spring, wheels, balance, etc., and the manner how they act on one another so as to make the needle point out the true time of the day."

The Arabs were once the continuators of the Greek tradition; they produced men of science. They have relapsed—all except those who are educated according to Western methods—into pre-scientific fatalism, with its attendant incuriosity and apathy. They are the "dull inquirers who, demanding an account of the phenomena of a watch, rest satisfied with being told that it is an engine made by a watchmaker." The result of their satisfaction with this extremely unsatisfactory answer is that their villages look like the ruins of villages, that the blow-flies sit undisturbedly feeding on the eyelids of those whom Allah has predestined to blindness, that half their babies die, and that, politically, they are not their own masters.

The Olive Tree

THE Tree of Life; the Bodhi Tree; Yggdrasil and the
Burning Bush:

> Populus Alcidae gratissima, vitis Iaccho,
> formosae myrtus Veneri, sua laurea Phoebo. . . .

Everywhere and, before the world was finally laicized,
at all times, trees have been worshipped. It is not to
be wondered at. The tree is an intrinsically "numinous" being. Solidified, a great fountain of life rises
in the trunk, spreads in the branches, scatters in a
spray of leaves and flowers and fruits. With a slow,
silent ferocity the roots go burrowing down into the
earth. Tender, yet irresistible, life battles with the un-
living stones and has the mastery. Half hidden in the
darkness, half displayed in the air of heaven, the tree
stands there, magnificent, a manifest god. Even to-day
we feel its majesty and beauty—feel in certain circumstances its rather fearful quality of otherness, strangeness, hostility. Trees in the mass can be almost terrible.
There are devils in the great pine-woods of the North,
in the swarming equatorial jungle. Alone in a forest
one sometimes becomes aware of the silence—the thick,
clotted, living silence of the trees; one realizes one's
isolation in the midst of a vast concourse of alien pres-

[291]

ences. Herne the Hunter was something more than the ghost of a Windsor gamekeeper. He was probably a survival of Jupiter Cernunnus; a lineal descendant of the Cretan Zeus; a wood god who in some of his aspects was frightening and even malignant.

> He blasts the tree, and takes the cattle,
> And makes milch-kine yield blood, and shakes a chain
> In a most hideous and dreadful manner.

Even in a royal forest and only twenty miles from London, the serried trees can inspire terror. Alone or in small groups, trees are benignly numinous. The alienness of the forest is so much attenuated in the park or the orchard that it changes its emotional sign and from oppressively sinister becomes delightful. Tamed and isolated, those leaping fountains of non-human life bring only refreshment to spirits parched by the dusty commerce of the world. Poetry is full of groves and shrubberies. One thinks of Milton, landscape-gardening in Eden, of Pope, at Twickenham. One remembers Coleridge's sycamore and Marvel's green thought in a green shade. Chaucer's love of trees was so great that he had to compile a whole catalogue in order to express it.

> But, Lorde, so I was glad and wel begoon!
> For over al, where I myn eyen caste,
> Weren trees, claad with levys that ay shal laste,
> Eche in his kynde, with colours fressh and grene
> As emerawde, that joy was for to sene.

[292]

The bylder oke, and eke the hardy asshe,
The peler (pillar) elme, the cofre unto careyne,
The box pipe tree, holme to whippes lasshe,
The saylynge firre, the cipresse deth to pleyne,
The sheter (shooter) ewe, the aspe for shaftes pleyne,
The olyve of pes, and eke the drunken vyne
The victor palme, the laurere, to, devyne.

I like them all, but especially the olive. For what it symbolizes, first of all—peace with its leaves and joy with its golden oil. True, the crown of olive was originally worn by Roman conquerors at ovation; the peace it proclaimed was the peace of victory, the peace which is too often only the tranquillity of exhaustion or complete annihilation. Rome and its customs have passed, and we remember of the olive only the fact that it stood for peace, not the circumstances in which it did so.

Incertainties now crown themselves assur'd,
And peace proclaims olives of endless age.

We are a long way from the imperator riding in triumph through the streets of Rome.

The association of olive leaves with peace is like the association of the number seven with good luck, or the colour green with hope. It is an arbitrary and, so to say, metaphysical association. That is why it has survived in the popular imagination down to the present day. Even in countries where the olive tree does not grow, men understand what is meant by "the olive branch" and can recognize, in a political cartoon, its

pointed leaves. The association of olive oil with joy
had a pragmatic reason. Applied externally, oil was
supposed to have medicinal properties. In the ancient
world those who could afford it were in the habit of
oiling themselves at every opportunity. A shiny and
well lubricated face was thought to be beautiful; it
was also a sign of prosperity. To the ancient Mediterranean peoples the association of oil with joy seemed
inevitable and obvious. Our habits are not those of the
Romans, Greeks and Hebrews. What to them was
"natural" is to-day hardly even imaginable. Patterns of
behaviour change, and ideas which are associated in
virtue of the pattern existing at a given moment of
history will cease to be associated when that pattern
exists no more. But ideas which are associated arbitrarily, in virtue of some principle, or some absence of
principle, unconnected with current behaviour patterns will remain associated through changing circumstances. One must be something of an archaeologist to
remember the old and once thoroughly reasonable association between olive oil and joy; the equally old,
but quite unreasonable and arbitrary association between olive leaves and peace has survived intact into
the machine age.

It is surprising, I often think, that our Protestant
bibliolaters should have paid so little attention to the
oil which played such an important part in the daily
lives of the ancient Hebrews. All that was greasy

possessed for the Jews a profound religious, social and
sensuous significance. Oil was used for anointing kings,
priests and sacred edifices. On festal days men's cheeks
and noses fairly shone with it; a matt-surfaced face
was a sign of mourning. Then there were the animal
fats. Fat meat was always a particularly welcome sacrifice. Unlike the modern child, Jehovah revelled in
mutton fat. His worshippers shared this taste. "Eat ye
that which is good," advises Isaiah, "and let your soul
delight itself in fatness." As for the prosperously wicked,
"they have more than their heart can wish" and the
proof of it is that "their eyes stand out with fatness."
The world of the Old Testament, it is evident, was
one where fats were scarce and correspondingly esteemed. One of our chief sources of edible fat, the pig,
was taboo to the Israelites. Butter and lard depend on
a supply of grass long enough for cows to get their
tongues round. But the pastures of Palestine are thin,
short and precarious. Cows there had no milk to spare,
and oxen were too valuable as draught animals to be
used for suet. Only the sheep and the olive remained
as sources of that physiologically necessary and therefore delicious fatness in which the Hebrew soul took
such delight. How intense that delight was is proved
by the way in which the Psalmist describes his religious experiences. "Because thy lovingkindness is better than life, my lips shall praise thee. . . . My soul
shall be satisfied as with marrow and fatness; and my

mouth shall praise thee with joyful lips." In this age of Danish bacon and unlimited margarine it would never occur to a religious writer to liken the mystical ecstasy to a good guzzle at the Savoy. If he wanted to describe it in terms of a sensuous experience, he would probably choose a sexual metaphor. Square meals are now too common to be ranked as epoch-making treats.

The "olyve of pes" is, then, a symbol and I love it for what it stands. I love it also for what it is in itself, aesthetically; for what it is in relation to the Mediterranean landscape in which it beautifully plays its part.

The English are Germans who have partially "gone Latin." But for William the Conqueror and the Angevins we should be just another nation of Teutons, speaking some uninteresting dialect of Dutch or Danish. The Normans gave us the English language, that beautifully compounded mixture of French and Saxon; and the English language moulded the English mind. By Latin out of German: such is our pedigree. We are essentially mongrels: that is the whole point of us. To be mongrels is our mission. If we would fulfil this mission adequately we must take pains to cultivate our mongrelism. Our Saxon and Celtic flesh requires to be constantly rewedded to the Latin spirit. For the most part the English have always realized this truth and acted upon it. From the time of Chaucer onwards almost all our writers have turned, by a kind of infallible instinct, like swallows, towards the South—towards the phantoms of Greece and Rome, towards the living realities of France and Italy. On the rare occasions when, losing their orientation, they have turned eastward and northward, the results have been deplorable. The works of Carlyle are there, an awful warning, to remind us of what happens when the English forget that their duty is to be mongrels and go whoring, within the bounds of consanguinity, after German gods.

The olive tree is an emblem of the Latinity towards which our migrant's instinct commands us perpetually to turn. As well as for peace and for joy, it stands for all that makes us specifically English rather than Teutonic; for those Mediterranean influences without which Chaucer and Shakespeare could never have become what they learned from France and Italy, from Rome and Greece, to be—the most essentially native of our poets. The olive tree is, so to speak, the complement of the oak; and the bright hard-edged landscapes in which it figures are the necessary correctives of those gauzy and indeterminate lovelinesses of the English scene. Under a polished sky the olives state their aesthetic case without the qualifications of mist, of shifting lights, of atmospheric perspective, which give to English landscapes their subtle and melancholy beauty. A perfect beauty in its way; but, as of all good things, one can have too much of it. The British Constitution is a most admirable invention; but it is good to come back occasionally to fixed first principles and the firm outline of syllogistic argument.

With clarity and definition is associated a certain physical spareness. Most of the great deciduous trees of England give one the impression, at any rate in summer, of being rather obese. In Scandinavian mythology Embla, the elm, was the first woman. Those who have lived much with old elm trees—and I spent a good part of my boyhood under their ponderous shade —will agree that the Scandinavians were men of insight. There is in effect something blowsily female about those vast trees that brood with all their bulging masses of foliage above the meadows of the home counties. In winter they are giant skeletons; and for a moment in the early spring a cloud of transparent emerald vapour floats in the air; but by June they have settled down to an enormous middle age.

By comparison the olive tree seems an athlete in training. It sits lightly on the earth and its foliage is never completely opaque. There is always air between the thin grey and silver leaves of the olive, always the flash of light within its shadows. By the end of summer the foliage of our northern trees is a great clot of dark unmitigated green. In the olive the lump is always leavened.

The landscape of the equator is, as the traveller discovers to his no small surprise, singularly like the landscape of the more luxuriant parts of southern England. He finds the same thick woods and, where man has cleared them, the same park-like expanses of luscious greenery. The whole is illumined by the same cloudy sky, alternately bright and dark, and wetted by precisely those showers of hot water which render yet more oppressive the sultriness of July days in the Thames valley or in Devonshire. The equator is England in summer, but raised, so to speak, to a higher power. Falmouth cubed equals Singapore. Between the equatorial and the temperate zone lies a belt of drought; even Provence is half a desert. The equator is dank, the tropics and the sub-tropics are predominantly dry. The Sahara and Arabia, the wastes of India and Central Asia and North America are a girdle round the earth of sand and naked rock. The Mediterranean lies on the fringes of this desert belt and the olive is its tree—the tree of a region of sun-lit clarity separating the damps of the equator from the damps of the North. It is the symbol of a classicism enclosed between two romanticisms.

"And where," Sir George Beaumont inquired of Constable, "where do you put your brown tree?" The reply was disquieting: the eccentric fellow didn't put it anywhere. There are no brown trees in Constable's landscapes. Breaking the tradition of more than a century, he boldly insisted on painting his trees bright green. Sir George, who had been brought up to think of English landscape in terms of raw Sienna and ochre, was bewildered. So was Chantrey. His criticism of Constable's style took a practical form. When "Hadleigh Castle" was sent to the Academy he took a pot of bitumen and glazed the whole foreground with a coat of rich brown. Constable had to spend several hours patiently scratching it off again. To paint a bright green tree and make a successful picture of it requires genius of no uncommon order. Nature is embarrassingly brilliant and variegated; only the greatest colourists know how to deal with such a shining profusion. Doubtful of their powers, the more cautious prefer to transpose reality into another and simpler key. The key of brown, for example. The England of the eighteenth-century painters is chronically autumnal.

At all seasons of the year the olive achieves that sober neutrality of tone which the deciduous trees of the North put on only in autumn and winter. "Where do you put your grey tree?" If you are painting in Provence, or Tuscany, you put it everywhere. At every season of the year the landscape is full of grey trees. The olive is essentially a painter's tree. It does not need to be transposed into another key, and it can be rendered completely in terms of pigment that are as old as the art of painting.

Large expanses of the Mediterranean scene are by Nature herself conceived and executed in the earth colours. Your grey tree and its background of bare bone-like hills, red-brown earth and the all but black cypresses and pines are within the range of the most ascetic palette. Derain can render Provence with half a dozen tubes of colour. How instructive to compare his olives with those of Renoir! White, black, *terra verde*—Derain's rendering of the grey tree is complete. But it is not the only complete rendering. Renoir was a man with a passion for bright gay colours. To this passion he added an extraordinary virtuosity in combining them. It was not in his nature to be content with a black, white and earth-green olive. His grey trees have shadows of cadmium green, and where they look towards the sun, are suffused with a glow of pink. Now, no olive has ever shown a trace of any colour warmer than the faint ochre of withering leaves and summer dusts. Nevertheless these pink trees, which in Renoir's paintings of Cagnes recall the exuberant girls of his latest, rosiest manner, are somehow quite startlingly like the cold grey olives which they apparently misrepresent. The rendering, so different from Derain's, is equally complete and satisfying.

If I could paint and had the necessary time, I should devote myself for a few years to making pictures only of olive trees. What a wealth of variations upon a single theme! Above Pietrasanta, for example, the first slopes of the Apuan Alps rise steeply from the plain in a series of terraces built up, step after step, by generations of patient cultivators. The risers of this great staircase are retaining walls of unmortared limestone;

the treads, of grass. And on every terrace grow the
olives. They are ancient trees; their boles are gnarled,
their branches strangely elbowed. Between the sharp narrow leaves one sees the sky; and beneath them in the thin
softly tempered light there are sheep grazing. Far off,
on a level with the eye, lies the sea. There is one picture, one series of pictures.

But olives will grow on the plain as well as on the
hillside. Between Seville and Cordoba the rolling
country is covered with what is almost a forest of olive
trees. It is a woodland scene. Elsewhere they are planted
more sparsely. I think, for example, of that plain at the
foot of the Maures in Provence. In spring, beside the
road from Toulon to Fréjus, the ploughed earth is a
rich Pozzuoli red. Above it hang the olives, grey, with
soft black shadows and their highest leaves flashing
white against the sky; and, between the olives, peach
trees in blossom—burning bushes of shell-pink flame
in violent and irreconcilable conflict with the red earth.
A problem, there, for the most accomplished painter.

In sunlight Renoir saw a flash of madder breaking
out of the grey foliage. Under a clouded sky, with rain
impending, the olives glitter with an equal but very
different intensity. There is no warmth in them now;
the leaves shine white, as though illumined from within
by a kind of lunar radiance. The soft black of the
shadows is deepened to the extreme of night. In every
tree there is simultaneously moonlight and darkness.

Under the approaching storm the olives take on another kind of being; they become more conspicuous in the landscape, more significant. Of what? Significant of what? But to that question, when we ask it, nature always stubbornly refuses to return a clear reply. At the sight of those mysterious lunar trees, at once so dark and so brilliant beneath the clouds, we ask, as Zechariah asked of the angel: "What are these two olive trees upon the right side of the candlestick and upon the left side thereof? What be these two olive branches which through the two golden pipes empty the golden oil out of themselves? And he answered me and said, Knowest thou not what these be? And I said, No, my lord. Then said he, These are the two anointed ones, that stand by the Lord of the whole earth." And that, I imagine, is about as explicit and comprehensible an answer as our Wordsworthian questionings are ever likely to receive.

Provence is a painter's paradise, and its tree, the olive, the painter's own tree. But there are disquieting signs of change. During the last few years there has been a steady destruction of olive orchards. Magnificent old trees are being cut, their wood sold for firing and the land they occupied planted with vines. Fifty years from now, it may be, the olive tree will almost have disappeared from southern France, and Provence will wear another aspect. It may be, I repeat; it is not certain. Nothing is certain nowadays except change. Even the majestic stability of agriculture has been shaken by the progress of technology. Thirty years ago, for example, the farmers of the Rhône valley grew rich on silkworms. Then came the invention of viscose. The caterpillars tried to compete with the machines and failed. The female form is now swathed in woodpulp, and between Lyons and Avignon the mulberry tree and its attendant worm are all but extinct. Vines were next planted. But North Africa was also planting vines. In a year of plenty *vin ordinaire* fetches about a penny a quart. The vines have been rooted up again, and to-day the prosperity of the Rhône valley depends on peach trees. A few years from now, no doubt, the Germans will be making synthetic peaches out of sawdust or coal tar. And then—what?

The enemy of the olive tree is the peanut. *Arachis hypogaea* grows like a weed all over the tropics and its seeds are fifty per cent. pure oil. The olive is slow-growing, capricious in its yield, requires much pruning, and the fruit must be hand picked. Peanut oil is half the price of olive oil. The Italians, who wish to keep their olive trees, have almost forbidden the use of peanut oil. The French, on the other hand, are the greatest importers of peanuts in Europe. Most of the oil they make is re-exported; but enough remains in France to imperil the olives of Provence. Will they go the way of the mulberry trees? Or will some new invention come rushing up in the nick of time with a

reprieve? It seems that, suitably treated, olive oil makes
an excellent lubricant, capable of standing up to high
temperatures. Thirty years from now, mineral lubri-
cants will be growing scarce. Along with the castor-oil
plant, the olive tree may come again triumphantly into
its own. Perhaps. Or perhaps not. The future of Provençal landscape is in the hands of the chemists. It is
in their power to preserve it as it is, or to alter it out
of all recognition.

It would not be the first time in the course of its
history that the landscape of Provence has changed its
face. The Provence that we know—terraced vineyard
and olive orchard alternating with pine-woods and those
deserts of limestone and prickly bushes which are
locally called garrigues—is profoundly unlike the Provence of Roman and mediaeval times. It was a land,
then, of great forests. The hills were covered with a
splendid growth of ilex trees and Aleppo pines. The
surviving Forêt du Dom allows us to guess what these
woods—the last outposts towards the south of the forests of the temperate zone—were like. To-day the garrigues, those end products of a long degeneration, have
taken their place. The story of Provençal vegetation is
a decline and fall, that begins with the ilex wood and
ends with the garrigue.

The process of destruction is a familiar one. The
trees were cut for firewood and shipbuilding. (The
naval arsenal at Toulon devoured the forest for miles

around.) The glass industry ate its way from the plain into the mountains, carrying with it irreparable destruction. Meanwhile, the farmers and the shepherds were busy, cutting into the woods in search of more land for the plough, burning them in order to have more pasture for their beasts. The young trees sprouted again—only to be eaten by the sheep and goats. In the end they gave up the struggle and what had been forest turned at last to a blasted heath. The long process of degradation ends in the garrigue. And even this blasted heath is not quite the end. Beyond the true garrigue, with its cistus, its broom, its prickly dwarf oak, there lie a series of false garrigues, vegetably speaking worse than the true. On purpose or by accident, somebody sets fire to the scrub. In the following spring the new shoots are eaten down to the ground. A coarse grass—baouco in Provençal—is all that manages to spring up. The shepherd is happy; his beasts can feed, as they could not do on the garrigue. But sheep and goats are ravenous. The new pasture is soon overgrazed. The baouco is torn up by the roots and disappears, giving place to ferocious blue thistles and the poisonous asphodel. With the asphodel the process is complete. Degradation can go no further. The asphodel is sheep-proof and even, thanks to its deeply planted tubers, fire-proof. And it allows very little else to grow in its neighbourhood. If protected long enough from fire and animals, the garrigue will gradually build itself up again into a forest. But a desert of asphodels obstinately remains itself.

Efforts are now being made to reafforest the blasted heaths of Provence. In an age of cigarette-smoking tourists the task is difficult and the interruptions by fire frequent and disheartening. One can hardly doubt, however, of the ultimate success of the undertaking. The chemists may spare the olive trees; and yet the face of Provence may still be changed. For the proper background to the olive trees is the thinly fledged limestone of the hills—pinkish and white and pale blue in the distance, like Cézanne's Mont Sainte Victoire. Reafforested, these hills will be almost black with ilex and pine. Half the painter's paradise will have gone, if the desert is brought back to life. With the cutting of the olive trees the other half will follow.

Set in Linotype Baskerville
Format by A. W. Rushmore
Manufactured by The Haddon Craftsmen
Published by HARPER & BROTHERS, *New York and London*